EDUCATIONAL AND ETHICAL LEADERSHIP - BEST PRACTICE

SAM ELDAKAK

authorHOUSE®

AuthorHouse™ LLC
1663 Liberty Drive
Bloomington, IN 47403
www.authorhouse.com
Phone: 1-800-839-8640

Published by AuthorHouse   03/21/2014

ISBN: 978-1-4918-9877-2 (sc)
ISBN: 978-1-4918-9878-9 (e)

Library of Congress Control Number: 2014905603

Any people depicted in stock imagery provided by Thinkstock are models,
and such images are being used for illustrative purposes only.
Certain stock imagery © Thinkstock.

This book is printed on acid-free paper.

Because of the dynamic nature of the Internet, any web addresses or
links contained in this book may have changed since publication and
may no longer be valid. The views expressed in this work are solely those
of the author and do not necessarily reflect the views of the publisher,
and the publisher hereby disclaims any responsibility for them.

Contents

Acknowledgments

I would like to extend my regards and appreciation to my research commettiee and supervisor. Their guidance and support were with me at every step. The chair of the committee, Dr. Donald Dunn, chair and members of the committee, Dr. Lorraine Cleeton and Professor, Saeed Askary. I also seek this opportunity to thank my beloved wife, Diane Monte for her support and encouragement. To my friends and collegues for their persistent support throughout my research. I am grateful for their believe in me. I also wish to thank them for their guidance without which accomplishing this study would never have been possible.

Abstract

Leadership and its concepts have been evolving since decades. There is a huge amount of extent literature defining and discussing the concepts and the traits associated with leaders and their effective leadership practices. In the contemporary world of today, the leaders and their practices are found to be influenced by the arising issues, evolving concepts, and formation of new values and principles in the current era. The current research study takes the task of exploring the challenges that organizational leaders face in the prescient world and how they cope with them to the best of their abilities. As this research adopts the Ethnography Primary Qualitative Research methodology therefore, ten organizational leaders were interviewed in order to gather their views about the characteristics of good leaders and their practices during ethical decision making. This research is an endeavor to contribute to the existing literature of leadership and its best practices.

CHAPTER 1: INTRODUCTION

In order to enhance the understanding of the current research this introductory chapter elucidates the background of the study first as well as to define the reasons that propel the researcher to conduct this study. The purpose of this chapter is to provide the readers of this study a brief overview about the research topic and to construct the main purpose and aim behind the research study. This chapter further comprises of the background of the research topic, statement of purpose, significance of the study, research aim, research objectives, research questions, and in the end an outline of the study. In the end, this chapter has outlined the dissertation structure enlightening the overall flow of each chapter and study. Also, key terms that have been used during the study have also been defined by the researcher precisely in this chapter.

Background of the Research Study

Leadership is a complex phenomenon. Fulmer and Conger (2004) illustrated that in the 21st century leadership is a focal area of research. The existing leadership research and literature tend to focus primarily on elucidating the behavior, characteristics and skills of effective and successful leaders. However, in the past decade, leadership has evolved into many forms and shapes. Leadership has been proffered for theoretical explanations throughout history. Kimbrough (2007) indicated that behavior of leaders is one facet of this change. Over the years a great number of definitions have been offered. Day (2000) stated that leadership is maintaining and creating a sense of culture, vision and interpersonal relationships. However, management is monitoring, supporting and coordinating the activities of an organization. In comparison to management leadership is a broader concept. The foundational aspects of business ethics are predicated on how effective a leader enables significant change in their organizations while retaining the most valuable aspects; culture, people, processes, and systems. Bolman, Crow, Goldring, Slater and Thurston (1994) reflected that people become leaders for the traits that they own such as appearance, intelligence and language ability etc. However, the recent approaches of Max Weber describe leadership trait as a focus on charisma and vision. Bolman and Deal (2003) categorized leadership into four frames as, political, human resource, symbolic and structural frames. However, effective leadership essence lies in knowing which frame to apply in particular situations that result in productive outcomes. Davis (1998) indicated that two significant elements of effective leadership are fostering positive interpersonal relationships and establishing a clear vision. A leader can foster positive interpersonal relationships and establish clear vision through effective leadership skills, attributes, and behavioral (Goldman, 1998). Decade over decade, leadership and leaders have been a significant concern of the research as well as literature in order to determine the key association of leaders and leadership to an organization success (Barnett, 2010). Therefore, the intent of the study is to ascertain how leadership sets the foundation for ongoing ethical compliance which become a catalyst for organizations to embrace ethnicity as a core value set, becoming part of its identity. In order to understand this and aspects of educational and ethical leadership leads it is indispensable to conduct this research.

Problem Statement

Leaders in an organization take the responsibility of gaining organization profit and meeting the ethical code of conduct. Bell (2005) noted that leaders have always been a source of motivation for employees as well as a catalyst for organization for better productivity, enhanced performance and profitability. Successful delivery of organization objectives and profits is dependent on the leaders' ability to develop smooth and collaborative relations with followers (Chan and Chan, 2005). Decision making itself is a challenging task for leaders as well as individuals and when it comes to Often leaders find difficulty in practicing their ethical code of conduct for making decisions due to the rigid organizational rules and others factors like values and principles, making decisions based on ethical code, the challenge becomes even more crucial. Leaders have to take care that their decision making must satisfy all ethical requirements with respect to individuals as well as the organization (Fulmer, 2004). Therefore, a leader must foresee the influence of his decision and must make sure that the decision is stratifying framework of the ethical code. The researcher in this study intends to identify the best practices of educational and ethical leadership for best outcomes for the individual as well as for the organization.

Research Aim and Objectives

The aim of this study is to ascertain educational and ethical Leadership—best practice. However, following objectives has been set by the researcher to achieve the set research aim.

1) To explore the characteristics of a good leader
2) To determine which forms of leadership are associated with educational effectiveness
3) To identify the difficulties faced by leaders during ethical decision making
4) To divulge the psychological and the social aspects that can endanger individual principals

Research Questions

Research questions in a study work as a guiding tool in assisting the researcher determine the key findings of the study that result in best outcomes and justify the research questions or hypotheses. However, the research questions for this study are as following:

1) What are the characteristics of good leaders?
2) Which forms of leadership are associated with educational effectiveness?
3) What are the difficulties faced by leaders during ethical decision making?
4) What are the psychological and the social aspects that can endanger individual principals?

Interview Questions

The interview questions that have been asked by the researcher from the participants of the study are as following:

1) How do you define leadership?
2) What are the characteristics of a good leader?
3) Which forms of leadership are associated with educational effectiveness?
4) What is the importance of ethics in decision-making in organizations?
5) What are the psychological and the social aspects that can endanger individuals' principles?

6) Describe your leadership traits in relation with integrity, honesty, and trustworthiness?
7) What in your opinion helps in dealing with ethical dilemmas during ethical decision making process?
8) What are the factors that affect your ethical decision making process?
9) How your personal values affect your decision making process?
10) What sort of difficulties do you experience during an ethical decision making process?
11) What piece of advice would you give to future leaders to be an effective leader?

Rationale of the Study

Management is what one does and a leader is one who leads (Avolio and Gardner, 2002). In terms of the ethnicity of any organization and its relationship to leadership, the foundations of leadership form a very solid foundation for driving ongoing change for the better on the dimension of ethnicity. The four dominant behavioral elements of leadership are specifically the building blocks of a highly ethical organizational structured (Avolio and Gardner, 2002). The first of these four elements are idealized influence, which is defined as the ability of a leader to create a very high level of trust with subordinates through charismatic leadership based on emotional intelligence (EI). Leaders have the ability to read potentially questionable ethical dilemmas quickly and accurately, and respond accordingly without sacrificing credibility or letting the company lapse into an ethical conflict (Jones, 1991). This aspect of leadership is what motivates subordinates to continually follow direction and seek to minimize the potential for unethical decision to be made in the first place.

The second aspect of leadership that is critically important for any leader to have a very strong level of inspirational motivation (Avolio and Gardner, 2002). This aspect of leadership is critically important for leaders set high expectations and get their subordinates, and in the case of CEOs, the entire company, to believe in their accomplishment. This is especially critical from an ethical leadership standpoint, as the norm has often become allowing small errors in ethics to be tolerated instead of questioning (Avolio and Gardner, 2002). A strong leader will be able to attain this level of performance by concentrating on their own behaviors as well, sending a clear message of what is appropriate in terms of ethical conduct (Miesing and Preble, 1985).

The third factor, intellectual stimulation, has to do with how effective a leader can challenge their subordinates to continually pursue challenging objectives even when the tasks associated with them are difficult. An example of this is when an organization must create a highly effective compliance program and the amount of time and rigor associated with it takes employees away from their primary jobs. An effective leader will be able to create enough interest in the program to continually show the value of compliance. The leaders in situations comparable to this also show very clearly how the financial rewards of being ethical, namely doing well is especially effective in illustrating how valuable ethnicity is. The intellectual stimulation aspect of this specific area of ethnicity as a corporate value emanate from also quantifying the value of being strong at Corporate Social Responsibility (CSR) for example, and the many benefits this aspect or attribute has to corporate performance. The ability of a leader to create intellectual stimulation also leads to a much higher level of credibility and trust as well (Jones, 1991).

The fourth factor that leaders rely on for creating a culture of ethnicity is an individualized consideration (Yukl, 1992). This is the ability to explain and show to each member of an organization what they value is and why their contribution is critical to the success of any initiative (Kouzes and Posner, 2002). This is crucial in any organization's direction on ethnicity and compliance, as change management is the most critical success factor there is in making large-scale changes in the culture of a company ((Avolio and Gardner, 2002). The ability to create a culture rich with individualized consideration will also serve as a very powerful catalyst for ongoing self-regulation on ethical challenges as well. The individualized consideration best practices continually show how leaders, when setting an example, often see their subordinates surpasses it in their own performance (Burke, 1999).

The ability of any organization to create a culture of strong ethnicity and compliance is driven by the leader's innate and learned strengths along the four dimensions of transformational leadership shown in this analysis (Paine, 1994). To the extent a leader models these values and also shows self-sacrifice in pursuit of an objective is the extent of ethical compliance in the short-run and ethnicity becoming a foundational element of the organizational culture over the long-term (Paine, 1994).

Scope of the Study

McCartney and Campbell (2006) indicated that leadership has always been a crucial subject of management for many years. Years after years several changes took place in the leadership styles, behavior and attitudes. However, its importance has always increased due to the increase in the competition and enhanced globalization (Heifetz, 1994). However, as this study is conducted for academic purpose, the researcher has not focused on leaders and leadership of any particular organization or sector. The researcher here has conducted the study understanding the best practices of educational and ethical leaders in general. In other words, the scope of this study is not limited. The findings of the study can be significantly used by the leaders of any sector and organization to enhance their leadership skills, behavior and attitude that may lead to productive outcomes.

Key Terms

In this paper, some ethical terms have been used to permit the readers to have a clear understanding of the definitions, as follows:

Transformational Leadership

Transformational leadership enhances the morale, motivation and performance of followers through a variety of mechanisms. These include connecting the followers self to the project, followers sense of identity and the collective identity of the organization that make them interested and inspires them to understand the strengths and weaknesses of followers and take greater ownership of their work so the leader enhance the performance.

Aspiration

Aspiration is defined as a goal or a desire in reaching a higher achievement.

Code of Conduct or Code of Ethics

Guides, rules, and regulations that support everyday decision-making process in order to make things clear to any organization's vision, mission, and values is the code of ethics or code of conduct. Those codes can be linked to as guidelines to the professional standards.

Conflict of Interest

When an individual interest clashes or collides with other interests.

Ethical Differences

A special situation where two people can justify their own decision making different from one another for the same value or a problem is referred as ethical difference.

Ethical Dilemmas

Facing a moral problem where moral judgment is required.

Ethics

The study of what is acceptable and not acceptable and what is wrong and what is right.

Integrity

Integrity is a decision-making process which is consistent with values and moral standards.

Moral values

Values that people believe in based on a society's interpretation to right versus wrong and good versus bad.

Task Force

Task force is creating a small group for a short period of time under one leader to complete a special objective.

Transparency

Act and practice clearly and straightforward in an open style.

Values

It's been an individual or a society's belief in what is right and important in life.

Limitation, Delimitation, and Assumption of the Study

Following limitation, delimitations and assumption were noted in this study.

Limitation of the Study

The following limitations exist in the study:
1) Some participants in this study may not represent or belong to the leadership team. They may be from the junior staff or belonging to the persons that may be assisting the team with administrative matters.
2) Gender of the participants in the research may limit the results.
3) Participants may not take the questions seriously.
4) Differences and inequality in participants' level of knowledge and experience

Delimitation of the Study

The following delimitations were noted in this study.
1) The majorities of the participants were from one higher level of leadership of males and there was a need for more decisive role of the other sex.
2) Some of the participants do not remember the organizations' visions, missions, and the core values.

Assumption of the Study

The following assumptions were noted in this study.
1) All participants were aware of the directions, clearly and openly. That goes against the delimitation of the study.
2) All participants were honest and straightforward about their knowledge and experience.
3) Research questions were related to the research topic accurately.

Research Design

Methodology is considered as the part of a research study that points out the ways and methods of compiling the data (Luthans and Avolio, 2003). Moreover, the literature of the study is based on secondary data. The study used document analysis as the primary method of data compilation. In the document analysis, the research study includes all types of academic studies, textual and multi-media products. Some of the data was compiled as a result of academic journals and online studies as well. The major aim of incorporation of such studies was to relate to the concepts identified in the paper to realize a working model. In addition, it was intended to make the research paper more methodical, too.

The following calculations will be selected to reach the objectives of the research:

1) Acquiring several organizational charts for few educational settings and calculate the standard and the level of management and leadership

2) Review current leadership practice and ethical decisions and moral values

3) The benchmarking is the process of constantly assessing the organizational goal processes and methodologies against other organizations, with the challenge of advancing and promoting its own performance. This comprises of setting goals and possible espousal of "best practices"-both internally and externally of the organization's industry.

4) The professionals in the quality-focused organizations understand that the quality incentive tools should motivate the organization to a better level of performance. These professionals must delineate those goals that are feasible to achieve and are meant to strive for continuous improvement in the organization.

Structure of the Dissertation

In this study, the researcher follow the standard framework of dissertation where the research study has been significantly divided into five distinct chapters each comprising of different content elucidating the methods, procedures and phases the researcher went through in order to acquire the best outcomes for the study under discussion. However, a brief overview of each chapter is as following:

The first chapter of the dissertation is *'Introduction'*. In this introductory chapter the research topic is introduced.

The second chapter of the dissertation is *'Literature Review'*. In this chapter previously conducted studies pertaining to the topic in chapter 1 are discussed.

In chapter 3, *'Methodology'* used for the research study is discussed in detail in order to provide the reader with an understanding of how the problem statement of the research is met.

Chapter four includes the *'Analysis and discussion'* of the research conducted according to chapter 3.

Finally in chapter 5, *'Conclusion and Recommendation'*, the entire work of the study is provided including topics and thoughts to be consider from the study and in recommended studies pertinent to the problem statement found in chapter 1.

CHAPTER 2:
REVIEW OF LITERATURE

This chapter reviews the literature that has been published in context of the topic of the study. The literature review for this study focuses on the effectiveness of leadership and the ethical decision making importance for an effective and competent leader in his or her organization by holding up the integrity and the principles of being an effective leader.

Literature on Leadership

According to Antonakis et.al (2004) the main focus of the research studies in the context of leadership revolves around finding out the nature of leadership and what the qualities of a successful and competent leader holds. Not significant amount of study has been conducted to explore the ethical decision making challenges faced by the leaders in their respective organization as the decision making process in any organization holds importance and is conducted in accordance with the nature and vision of the organization. In 2008, Kimberling pointed out an important fact regarding this aspect of leadership that the leaders associated with public sector organizations have not been able to sustain the trust of the public in their credibility and honesty as a reason of the scandals of unethical behavior. Gibelman and Gelman (2000) stared the same findings in their study regarding the unethical and self-seeking behavior on the part of the leaders. Their study accused the leaders with self-centered reasons for the decisions they make.

Theoretical Framework

It could easily be said that a number of certain external and internal factors influence the ethical decision making process of leaders in their organizations. These factors have been established over time and have influenced the ethical values and principles of the leader and guided their practice (Polkinghorne, 2005). The experiences of the leaders and their personal ethics are the driving force that guides the process of their decision making (Burns, 2004). This was a qualitative study that used the transformational theory of leadership.

Trustworthy leadership came in as a discipline of leadership and had the concepts that covered the extended boundaries of leadership theories and practices (Avolio & Gardner, 2005). The vertical dyad theory was refined and then came to be known as leader-member exchange theory. The theories and the practices devised for the leaders have become ever so important for successful leadership.

According to Avolio & Gardner, (2005) genuine leadership is carried out through incorporating trustworthiness, truthfulness and integrity as an essential part of behavior and practices. As George (2003) opined that an organization always needs leaders with high integral principles and values that make them committed to the vision and the mission of the organization. Many researchers have opined that the decision making process highlights the qualities and integrity of a leader in true sense. That is the reason that trustworthy leadership enhances ethical leadership (Resick et al., 2006).A trustworthy leader is a person whom people can trust and rely on for having responsible, sensible and sincere guidance. Therefore, according to these theories this attributes to the fact that if a leader is responsible and has the discussed characteristics, then he is capable of making ethical decisions for sure (Ciulla, 2003). The success of organizations and the educational institutions depends on the personal constructs of the individuals who lead them. As said by (Waggoner, 2010) individual credibility and competency of a person is critical to the success of the organization.

Ethical Decision Making in Leadership

The responsibility of chalking ethical principles to be followed in an organization lies on the shoulders of leaders. It is a general rules that the ethical code of conduct, as set by the leaders is supposed to be followed in making all organizational decisions. Ethics of a person is marked with the influence of surroundings, parents, educational leaders and teachers in the early childhood years. This early knowledge about ethics decides the potential of making decisions with in the ethical code. Apart from the knowledge about ethics, there are certain other factors which influence the decision making. These factors involve organizational environment, government policies and sometimes spiritual beliefs. Ethical code defines the behavior that must be practiced in an organization to uphold moral values like tolerance, integrity and collaboration. Ethical decisions depend on those ethical values which are being practiced in routine activities. Social and psychological aspects influence ethical decisions in more significant way than the economical aspect.

Trevino, et.al (1999) considers that sometimes organizations define their own set of principles regarding ethics which directly influence decision making. Delaney &Sockell (1992) state that a number of attempts have been made in order to guide leaders about the process of decision making in accordance with the ethical code of conduct. It is necessary to guide leaders particularly about ethical decision making because they influence organizational human resources in the most significant way. Trevino & Brown (2004) point the fact that it is very important for organizations to make sure that leaders are not misusing their authority of guiding others about ethical decisions.

Beasley &Hermanson (2004) emphasize the importance of defining policies and guidelines about code of conduct in organizations by quoting the fact that the failures in ethical decision making have been causing damage to the integrity of organization. Lunday& Barry (2004) that although leaders are responsible to guide others about decision making in accordance with ethics but it also depends on individuals' behavior and knowledge about ethics. Harvey (2001) states that the potential of making ethical decisions depends significantly on childhood knowledge about ethics but guidelines and leadership also influence the potential of making ethical decisions.

Important Factors influencing the ethical decision-making process

According to Kohlberg (1969) defines ethics as behavior and actions of a person which he takes in order to fulfill the demands of the society. At the same time Beauchamp & Bowie (2004) that ethics means the knowledge and set of principles guide individuals to distinguish between the right and wrong. Keeping in view these definitions of ethics, it is clear that the process of ethical decision making depends on a number of social, environmental and personal factors. These factors play a decisive role in understanding the knowledge behind the guidelines of ethics. There is a clear difference between the failures of ethical decisions and having inadequate knowledge about ethics. Numerous studies suggest that the best way to have clear understanding and knowledge about ethics and ethical decision making is to study those factors which influence the ethical decision making process. These factors may be moral, social or psychological depending upon the environment and scenario. Trevino & Brown (2004) suggest that guidelines about ethical decision making must be defined by avoiding any emotional aspect. Emotional behaviors affect the values and priorities of a person. The study of Trevino & Brown also suggest that the knowledge about factors which influence the potential of ethical decision making also assists in a focused assessment about the guidelines and ethical decisions. Leaders must have a clear knowledge about ethics and how social and psychological factors influence the decision making process. Ethical decision making of leaders set an example for others to follow. Kouzes & Posner (2002) mark ethical knowledge as the most important factor required for effective and successful leadership. The most significant and considerable aspect of leadership is making decisions in accordance with the ethical code of conduct.

For the integration of an organization, leaders who understand the value of ethical decision making are very important. Ciulla (2004) define the dire need of effective leaders by all organizations as the lack of such leaders who have potential of making ethical decisions. The in-depth and detailed study of Kouzes and Posner (2002) supports the perception that human resources in an organization need the leadership which can uphold the values of integrity and ethics. The ethical knowledge of leaders serves the purpose of guiding and training their followers about ethical decision making. One of the most challenging factors which put leaders into real test is the organizational competition. In such demanding situations leaders have to utilize their capability of ethical decision making in order to meet all the competitive demands without violating code of conduct. The study of Badaracco (2002) says that such situations determine the capability of leaders to make decisions which do not demoralize ethical values and at the same time favor the benefit of the organization.

The factors which influence the capability of ethical decision making may be categorized as internal and external factors. The forces prevailing within the organization constitute the internal factors while those present outside the organization define external factors. According to the research of Bischoff & Karri (2002) the combination of these factors reflects the psychology of a person about the assessment of circumstances. Kelley & Elm (2003) and Polkinghorne (2005) also support this idea by stating that the optimism and clarity in the approach of a person, as determined by external and internal factors, influence the ethical decision making capabilities of a person. Whereas Burns (2004) suggests that ethics of a person are not significantly influenced by organizational factors but ethical decision making depends on the individual knowledge and understanding about ethics. The knowledge about ethics lays the basis of ethical decision making, according to Burns.

Apart from research studies there are number of theories which define set of principles and guidelines about the procedure of making ethical decisions. Kohlberg (1976) says that it is very important for leaders to observe the significance of values in order to obey the code of conduct. Jones' (1991) proposed a model which suggested that in the course of resolving issues, leaders may face certain challenges which can affect their ethical decisions. Bennis (1984) says that it is very important for leaders to implement their knowledge about ethics in routine activities. This is necessary to effectively guide followers about the dealing challenging circumstances by making ethical decisions. Sankar (2003) emphasizes on the influence of spiritual beliefs on decision making in accordance with ethical code. This is so because moral values and their priorities vary with difference of religious education as well.

Importance of Ethical Decision Making

The importance of ethical decision making of leaders is emphasized by a number of studies and theories. Christen and Kohls (2003) in their study highlight the importance of ethical decision making particularly in emergency scenarios. The study marks ethical decision making as the tool of coping with the challenges of emergencies. It also serves the purpose of assuring stakeholders in the state of problem. Gini (2004) says that ethical values guide about maintaining a balance between the needs of individuals and organization. According to Bell (2005) the literal meaning of the words Ethics elaborates its importance in the decision making process for leaders particularly. The word Ethic is originated from a reek terminology 'Ethos' which means behavior. According to this study, the behavior of a leader in critical situations determines the behavior of followers which ultimately influences the integrity of the organization. The vision about right and wrong defines the ethics of a person. The capability of making decisions based on ethical values and the approach to handle a situation depends on how much a person values principles and morality.

Burns (2004) categorizes ethics in leaders into different groups depending on priorities and requirements of an organization. This study suggests that ethics cover all moral values like kindness, sincerity, tolerance, integrity, genuine character. When all these values are unite together then they form the guidelines of ethical decisions. According to Burns, ethics also guide about maintaining relations with other individuals. An ethical leader influences his followers due to moral values which are being reflected in routine activities. Burns says that although priorities and requirements influence the procedure of ethical decision making but values like equality, organization and justice. Burn's study also highlights the importance of focusing the factors which may influence the decisions based on ethical code of conduct. Ciulla (2004) says that the effectiveness of leadership mainly revolves around ethics and its guidelines. An ethical leader leaves a deep and long lasting influence on his followers.

According to the study conducted by Rest (2004), challenges regarding ethics are not limited to a particular organizational level. The study suggests that the delicacy of ethical decision increases as the hierarchy of the organization ascends. This is due to the complexity involved in maintaining balanced relations with individuals as well as with organizations. Therefore at the level of leadership, ethical decision making s most critical. The study of Rest says that in some challenging situations ethical decisions make a leader to choose between the organizational interest and obeying the ethical guidelines. The violation of ethical code of conduct may result in demoralized acts like fluff, deceit etc.

The research of Rhode and Packel (2009) further clarifies the importance of ethical decision making by analyzing the four most significant factors which influence the capability of leaders to make ethical decisions. The first factor is the realization and marking those causes which give rise to ethically challenging situations. The second factor which id the capability of a leader to choose the best way in which a critical situation can be dealt with in the ethical limits. Third factor, according t this research is the knowledge about ethics and code of conduct which sets the priorities of a leader for making ethical decisions. The fourth factor is the leadership skills which decide the strategy through which an ethical decision should be executed. Rhode and Packel also say that the most delicate sector where the probability of demoralization of ethical values is very high is usually the financial sector of an organization.

Weston (2001) defines ethics as a set of guiding principles of moral values which reflect the personal views f an individual about the choice of right and wrong. The study of Weston signifies ethics by highlighting the fact that ethical decision serves as a tool to optimize the organizational profits by defining a guideline to the human resources which they have to flow while taking any decision. This assures integrity and collaborative environment. Bennis (2000) and Burke (1999) say that to ensure that the code of conduct id being followed, ethical leadership is necessary. Ethical decisions of a leader pave a way to the practical implementation of ethical guidelines and code of conduct. Carlson, Kacmar & Wadsworth (2002) say that the importance of ethical decisions for an organization cannot be denied at any point but ethical values of every leader vary with his insight about morality.

Challenges for leaders

There is no denial to the fact that ethical decisions influence the effectiveness of leadership in a very positive way but there are certain challenges that leaders face while making ethical decisions. Leadership is the level where maintaining a balance between ethical values and organizational profits is very critical. A simple decision of choosing between right and wrong within the ethical code becomes a challenge sometimes. Bird (2005) suggest that the environment of organization and level of demoralization of ethical values pose a great challenge for leaders in making decisions following ethical code. Bird's study also points the fact that the scenario where violation of ethical code is obvious is very often encountered and when leaders take actions to rectify this flaw, they are considered as a threat to the benefits of the organization. Another challenge, according to Bird's study, is the conflict in views on leadership level which results in the disintegration of followers. This difference in opinion hinders a leader to make decisions according to ethical code.

The study conducted by Burke (2006) says that the effectiveness of leadership also acts as a challenge in the process of ethical decision making by a leader. If a leader is unable in developing smooth and collaborative relations with followers then successful delivery of education about ethical decision making will not be possible. Burke (2006) says that ethical guidelines about decision making covers delicate aspects like values and morality therefore communication between leader and followers must be smooth. Weaver (2007) also quote the fact that lack of interpersonal skills is one of the biggest challenges for leaders in giving effective education to followers about making decisions according to ethical code. Their study says that it is one of the most frequently encountered issues by the leaders. McCartney and Campbell further explain that those leaders who encountered this problem usually fail in maintaining balance among a number of aspects at the same time which is the essence of successful ethical decision making. Another challenge for leaders is effective team work. Those leaders, who have the ability to assist and guide the team members in adjusting with the requirements of a team, can effectively play their roles as leaders.

Rhode and Packel (2009) say that organizational policies may overlook the importance of ethical decision making due to profit oriented approach. This creates another challenging situation for those leaders who practice ethical values in making decisions. A number of organizations ensure the compliance of organizational polices with ethical code but due to the increasing competition in the market most of the organizations prioritize profit even at the cost of violation of ethical code of conduct. Rhode and Packel (2009) further explain that this challenging situation can be dealt with mandatory law enforcement in organizations. This would help in establishing defined codes for every venture and project maintaining a balance between ethical decisions and organizational profit. These defined policies will also help in resolving conflicts among leaders. The integrity among leaders would ultimately affect the organization in a profitable way. Cohan (2004) highlighted the other side of the picture. According to this study, underestimating the importance of ethical decisions hinder effective leadership but at the same time overestimating the importance of ethics can also put too much pressure on leaders to play their role effectively. There are number of studies which highlight the fact that formulation of ethical code does not ensure the implementation of ethics in decision making and other activities. In such situations leaders feel pulled in two opposite directions which impact their skills and decision making capabilities.

Ostrower (2007) explains this challenging situation of implementing ethical codes in organizations as the inflexible formulation of policies and codes which focus only some limited aspects. Rhode and Packel (2009) say that leaders find difficulty in practicing their ethical code of conduct for making decisions due to the rigid organizational rules. One of such rules is the penalty payment for violating any policy formed by the administration. Such rigid rules restrict leaders to only practice those ethical codes which are in favor of the organization. In such circumstances there is a probability that leadership cannot be effective enough to influence followers for practicing ethical decision making. Rhode and Packel (2009) suggest that in order to eradicate the prevailing conflict between the formulation and implementation of ethical code, organizations should be educated about the measures needed to be taken for the practical implementation of ethical code of conduct particularly in decision making.

Kotter (2007) says that decision making itself is a challenging task for leaders as well as individuals and when it comes to making decisions based on ethical code, the challenge becomes even more crucial. Leaders have to take care that their decision making must satisfy all ethical requirements with respect to individuals as well as the organization. They have to fulfill dual responsibilities simultaneously keeping in mind that their decision making does not result in ethical challenges. Kotter highlights the fact that sometimes leaders take an ethical decision but the decision might result in unethical consequences. Therefore a leader must foresee the influence of his decision and must make sure that the decision is stratifying framework of the ethical code. In the same study Kotter says that ethical decision making always favor an organization because the influence of ethical leaders simultaneously impresses employers and motivate the followers to practice the same code of conduct which ensures mutual understanding and integrity.

Kotter (2007) also says that ethics among leader serve as a driving force for organizations and human resources to practice ethical code of conduct in all activities.

The difference of opinion between different sectors of an organization also creates a challenging situation for leaders. Effective leadership revolves around ethics. An ethical leader guides followers to practice the same code of conduct which ultimately reduces difference in point of views. Organizations where rigidness in behavior of higher hierarchy reins supreme, leaders cannot unite all under a single platform to practice a single ethical code of conduct. Apart from posing challenges for leaders, this also affects the productivity of the organization in an adverse way due to disintegration and deteriorating moral values. The study of Blakeley (2007) says that another challenge for leaders is their own potential to make decisions satisfying ethical code of conduct. The capability of a leader to make ethical decisions reflect his knowledge and insight about ethics. Therefore overcoming the flaws in decision making is itself a big challenge for leaders. The decisions made by leaders influence the organizations and individuals simultaneously. Leaders set guidelines for individuals for practicing ethical code of conduct and any flaw in the decision making can impact individual's perspective about ethical decision making. Therefore the inability of leaders to realize and rectify those causes which are making the leadership flawed and ineffective is a challenge in making ethical decisions. It is therefore emphasized by a number of researchers to conduct training programs for leaders to meet all the challenges of effective and ethical leadership.

Ethical Decision Making in the light of Theories

A number of theories support the procedure of ethical decision making and support the fact that ethical decision covers a number of aspects simultaneously and there is no single code of conduct which defines every approach of ethical decision. Approaches of ethical decision vary with the knowledge and insight about ethics and also with the nature of scenario. Trevino (1987) says that although there are a number of approaches of making decisions in accordance with the ethical code of conduct. Christensen &Kohls (2003) emphasize on the need of education programs about ethical decision making for leaders as well as for individuals in order to broaden their vision about ethics. Wood and Bandura (1989) in their cognitive theory cover social, environmental and individual aspects which influence the decision making capability. This theory also emphasizes that these factors must be kept in mind while designing the ethical code of conduct. This theory focuses the cognitive behavior of individuals in a social set up. The priorities, actions and behavior of individuals vary with the varying social circumstances. Therefore, cognitive theory supports a flexible ethical framework which can adjust these variations in decision making approaches. Jung (2002) says that the influence of cultural aspects decides the approach that should be adopted in making ethical decisions. Trevino & Brown (2004) express that the assessment of a decision varies with insights of individuals but the fact that must be considered is the influence of the decision on all. If the decision satisfies all ethical concerns then individuals' assessment does not matter. According to Kohlberg (1976) ethical decisions can not only influence others but it can also alter one's own social perspective. Many of the researchers and theories support the fact that social aspects and gatherings can significantly influence the approach of making ethical decisions.

Ford & Richardson (1994) and Fritzsche, (1995) suggest that there are limited research which analyze the factors and significance of ethical decision making. The social and psychological aspects affect the procedure of ethical decision making in the most influential way. Green (2005) draws the conclusion based on his clinical experience that human psychology reflects the early years of learning and this psychology decides the potential of making decisions. As far as decisions in accordance with ethics are concerned then they depend on the knowledge and environment provided in early period of childhood. Christensen and Kohls (2003) say that there are certain ethical decisions which may put an organization in a challenging situation. It depends on the code of conduct practiced in the organization that whether the organization supports ethical decisions or violate code of conduct for organizational benefits. If the organization favors violation of ethical decisions for the sake of benefits then it means that only a specific group of managers is empowered to make decisions without following ethical code. Christensen and Kohls suggest that such scenarios suppress the importance of ethics and moral values and organization suffers for disintegration due to biased and ineffective leadership. This creates an aura of monopoly where leaders with potential of making ethical decisions are underestimated.

According to Aaltio-Marjosola & Takala (2000) and Bennis (2004), there are number of studies which highlight the fact that organizations as well as individuals are influenced by the effective and ethical leaders. Caldwell et al. (2002) and Trevino et al. (2000) also support this evidence by stating that the ethical decisions made by leaders reflect their potential of coping with challenges within ethical limits. An ethical leader leaves a long lasting influence on his followers. Conger &Kanungo (1987) and Conger, Kanungo, & Menon (2000) express that apart from influencing followers, ethical values also add charisma which serves as powerful motivational tool for a leader to draw the attention of his followers. In addition to it, ethical leader can interact with followers in an effective way by showing tolerance and dignity (Aaltio-Marjosola & Takala, 2000; Trevino & Brown, 2004; Trevino et al., 2000). An effective leader can guide the followers to act in accordance with the designed framework of code of conduct. An ethical leader can adopt different approaches to motivate followers toward implying ethics in all activities including decision making. Yukl & Tracey (1992) the action and decision making capabilities of followers is the direct measure of the effectiveness and skills of an ethical leader.

Weston (2001) expresses that an effective leader has a very strong interpersonal connection with the followers and Aaltio-Marjosola & Takala (2000) say that this interpersonal association can be utilized in enhancing the personal as well as organizational skills of followers. Apart from being effective, leaders must be ethical in order to utilize the skills of followers with in ethical limits and guide them to deal with challenges of business in an ethical way rather than misusing the potential of followers in order to enhance the business profit. Aaltio-Marjosola & Takala (2000) states that the motivational force of an effective leader makes followers to realize their own potential and skills. Sometimes it can create a complex situation for organizations as an unethical but effective leader can create own ally which can pose a threat to the integrity of the organization. Therefore all theories emphasize that ethics of a leader assure the integrity of followers and organizations.

Importance of Obedience in Ethical Decisions and Milgram's Study

The study conducted by Milgram in 1963 focuses particularly on the element of obedience in the ethical code. This study suggests that followers' obedience to their leader can be utilized in controlling the actions and behaviors of individuals. The study reflects the importance of ethics in order to use the obedience of follower in right direction. An effective but unethical leader can exploit the obedience of followers by manipulating their beliefs and ability to analyze the difference between wrong and right. An ethical leader utilizes the obedience of followers in enhancing their skills of decision making and acting on the guidelines of ethical decision making as set by their leader. Milgram's study defines obedience as the key to control the psychology of the follower. It depends on ethics of the leader that how this obedience is being utilized.

Milgram's study is based on engaging participants in an experiment to make them realize that exploitation of obedience can result in loss of ability to think. Milgarm clarified to the participants that the aim of the experimental study is to emphasize the importance of ethical leadership for followers. An unethical leader considers followers' obedience as their will to let him control them. Whereas an ethical leader to consider the obedience of follower as their will to understand and act on the guiding principles of ethical decision making. The study of Milgram aimed at making the participants realize that obedience in ethical code of conduct can educate them to make their own decisions based on ethical code of conduct.

Milgram conducted an experiment to test the impact of unethical utilization on the obedience of followers. Milgram gathered 40 participants and out them into a test. He asked them to bear shocks from an electrical instrument. Despite the awareness about adverse effect of electric shocks, participants continued to obey the orders. Milagram took the experiment to the next level in order to determine the limit to which an unethical leader can exploit an obedient follower. Out of 40 participants, 26 continued to obey the order of raising shock level. Although they knew that this can endanger their lives, they trusted their leader and ignored their own point of view. This experiment aimed at highlighting the importance if an ethical leader for utilizing the obedience of followers in an effective way.

The conclusion of Milgram's study suggests that there are certain requirements which must be kept in mind for making effective and optimistic use of obedience. The most important factor which should be analyzed is the ethical code of the leader. Other factors are compliance of followers' actions in with legal policies of the organization and the need of the action to be taken. An ethical leader utilizes the obedience of followers in fulfilling the organizational duties. On the other hand an unethical leader tries to control the voluntary actions of followers due to their trust and obedience. The study highlights the fact that being effective is not enough for a leader but it is also very important that the leader possesses knowledge about ethics and ethical decision making.

Correlation between Moral Intensity and Ethical Decisions

Jones (1991) in his study correlated moral values and ethical decisions. According to this study, the decision making process based on ethics is directly concerned with the moral values of a person. The theme of this study reflects that the idea that the strength of morality effects the procedure of ethical decision making as well as the decision maker itself. He proposed that the strength of morality has a direct relation with the relationship of leader with followers. As the morality started getting intense, the influence of ethical decisions of a leader on his relation with individuals starts increasing. This is because the degree of morality shows the inside of a person and reflects his ethical beliefs. Kelley and Elm (2003) further researched on this theory and drew the conclusion that a leader with intense moral values always form intense decisions and the intensity of his ethical decision is directly concerned with the framework of an organization. Kelley and Elm noted that organizations which have a solid and defined framework influence the ethical decisions of a leader.

Influence of Spirituality on Ethical Decisions

According to Fort (1996, 1997) the influence of religion and religious beliefs on ethical decisions cannot be denied at any point. Weber (1930) suggested that when spiritual beliefs are ignored in the process of making decisions then the procedure starts resembling with a game. Weber says that making decisions in the basis of ethics requires unambiguous knowledge about ethics and ethical education is directly linked with religion.

Miesing & Preble (1985) and Siu, Dickinson, & Lee (2000) agree with the fact that all religions promote moral and ethical values therefore there is certainly a high probability that the ethics of a person reflect his religious beliefs. Weston (2001) emphasized the importance of religious influence by stating that the best knowledge of ethics can be delivered by a religion. At the same time Weston also states the fact that religious beliefs confine the approach and thinking capacity of a person in a particular direction. Although religion promotes ethics but it also reduces the flexibility in the approach of a person. As a result of this rigidness in the approach, the ethical decisions made by such a person usually reflect extreme consequences. Ethical decisions need simultaneous analysis of different aspects but religious beliefs drive the observation of a person to a single direction. Whereas ethical education based on general realization of good and bad always provides more space to think and understand the logic behind a principle.

A research based on the survey of 850 students support the conclusions of these studies about the influence of religion on ethical decision making capabilities. Those students who studied in a religious educational institute declared that religion set a complete code of conduct and all ethical values are taught by religious beliefs. On the other hand those students who studied in a modern educational institute said that ethical decision making is more linked with the moral character of a person than with the religious beliefs. They said that two persons believing the same religion can have different ethical insights. This difference in the approaches of students reflects their perspective about religious beliefs and decision making.

Pillars of Ethical Decision Making

Bennis and Thomas (2002) say that in the list of values, integrity always tops the list of ethical values. For an effective leader maintaining a balance between social aspects and individual requirements is very important. Integrity is the pillar of ethical code of conduct which assists a leader in maintaining balanced relationships and also motivates the leader to uphold moral values in daily activities. Their study also quotes the fact that integrity is such a value which is noticed by others in a considerable way. Integrity in a leader serves as the most effective tool to develop trust of followers and others. When integrity becomes an essential element of the personality then every personal activity reflect integrity an ethics. Paine (1994) says that integrity in the behavior of leaders can serve as a strategic tool in making ethical decisions. When an organizational framework is based in the principles of integrity then the ethical code formulated, guides all individuals to carry on their activities and make decisions in an ethical way.

The general perceptions and definitions of honesty suppress the importance of honesty in the ethical decision making and promoting smooth interaction with other individuals. Smith (2003) says that honesty eradicates the conflict between the words and actions of a person; therefore an honest leader draws the attention of followers in an effective way. Fritzsche (1995) and Parry & Proctor-Thomson (2002) declare honesty as one of the most important components which influence ethical decisions of leaders. Trevino & Brown (2004) that honesty in the actions of a person ensures the high morality of a leader and therefore the decisions made by honest leaders reflect their integral behavior. Vitell (2000) conducted a survey among 527 organizations for analyzing the importance of ethical decision making in these organizations. The survey was also conducted to determine the importance of honesty for making ethical decisions.

The results of the survey reflected that most of the companies who took part in the survey showed that despite the ethical framework, companies have encountered ethical confrontations with clients. Half of the companies agreed that due to the deterioration in the worth of ethical values, ethical issues have become more crucial with time. A number of companies also reported that ethical framework plays a vital role in ethical decision making process for leaders. Due to the increased competition and the importance of ethical values is ignored while making decisions. Almost all the companies participated in the competition agreed to the fact that the evolving market competition has changed the priorities of organizations in forming ethical framework. The survey concludes the fact that the declining value if ethical decisions id due to the reduced importance of honesty in the actions of leaders.

According to Kouzes & Posner (2002) and Yukl (1989), for a smooth and interactive relation between a leader and the follower, trust is the most important factor. Trust of followers in their leader helps in earning their obedience and also in acting on the guidelines as set by their trusted leader. Christen and Kohls (2003) say that although it is the duty of followers to obey their leaders but when followers trust their leaders then it assists in transforming the perceptions and ethical behavior of followers. Beu and Buckley (2001) there is no space for demoralized acts in the relations between a leader and its followers based on trust. Brewer (1997) says that the importance of trust in a relation can be analyzed by those leaders who have sound knowledge about ethics and understand the value of ethics in maintaining a collaborative environment. Trust keeps on strengthening as leaders continue to act in accordance with the ethical code of conduct. A number of studies have considered trust as an essential component f making ethical decisions.

The cognitive theory of Kohlberg's (1969) suggests that when it comes to the assessment of a leader by followers then trusts plays an essential role in justifying the ethical behavior of leaders. Judging the moral values of a leader is based on two vital factors. The first factor is the personal insight of followers about ethics and the scenario in which the decision is made.

Reidenbach and Robin (1990) that assessment of ethical leaders is based on the same three pillars in which ethical behavior is based that is honesty, trust and integrity. The strength of these pillars depends on the early years of learning and knowledge provided by parents and surroundings. The practical implication of ethical values in daily activities is learnt through experiences regarding coping with social and cultural challenges. The awareness about the importance of ethical decision making plays a vital role in acting in accordance with the ethical code of conduct in daily organizational activities. Morality of the leader directly affects the potential of decision making on the basis of ethical code of conduct. Considerable factors which influence the capabilities of a leader in making ethical decisions covers social, psychological, legal, organizational and personal aspects. The study of Reidenbach and Robin (1990) says that the judgment of followers about ethics of a leader varies with scenarios, and personal reasons.

D'Aprix (2005) quotes that the personal knowledge and insight of deciding about good and bad play a major role in making ethical decisions. Leaders also have freedom in choosing the method of judgment of ethical decisions in accordance with the circumstances. Leaders can also utilize their insight about coping with organizational challenges in accordance with the designed framework of the organization. Flawed beliefs and inadequate knowledge about ethics may result in the biased behavior f the leader in dealing with a problem. Usually the utilization of general perception about right and wrong is considered as unreliable in making ethical decisions. At the same time it should be noted that most of the leaders utilize their general knowledge about wrong and right in making ethical decisions. Here general perception refers to the state of knowledge which is free of ethical or spiritual influences. Although solely general knowledge is considered as unreliable but at the same time it plays a significant role in determining the ethical decision making capabilities of a leader.

Leadership in Education

Educational institutes decide the future of individuals as well as of the country. Begley (2001) conducted the study in the basis of authentic pieces of literature on the importance of effective leadership and ethical decision making in educational filed. The study of Begley quotes the fact that educational institutes are delicate sectors therefore it is very important to observe the importance of effective and ethical leaders in education. Educational years contribute in the formulation of moral character of a person. Therefore the need of an ethical leader serves as the basic requirement for providing ethical education to students. There is a direct influence of society and surroundings in the relationship of leader and followers. The study also points towards the fact that there is no significant literature provided on professional as well as personal aspects of effective leadership. This study says that often the boundaries between personal and professional ethical aspects are ignored and are treated as a single set of principles.

Begley and Leithwood (1990) study is based on the survey among 15 administrators of educational institutes. This survey was conducted in order to examine the importance of ethics for administrators in the formulation of educational policies. The study also aimed at rectifying the flawed approach of considering educational leaders as ethics free leaders. The result of the survey indicated that most of the administrators ignore the importance of ethical code of conduct in education and form policies and strategies on the basis of personal perspectives. The study of Leithwood and Stager (1989) is also a survey based study and it indicates that administrators and educational leaders rely on their personal vision about moral values in two cases. Either they do not have sufficient knowledge about ethical decision making or they encounter a unique scenario where they do not know about how to implement ethical code of conduct to resolve the problem.

Educational Ethical Decisions

Begley and Leithwood (1990) in their research stated that the moral and ethical values influence the educational decisions in a direct way. In order to determine those aspects which are being influenced by the ethical decision making Begley and Leithwood investigated 39 educational leaders about the importance of ethics in educational decision making. The knowledge about ethical decision making is very important for educational leaders in order to determine the conflicts between formulation and implementation of educational policies. This is also important to maintain a balance between inter-organizational policies and social aspects. The study also emphasized on the need of authentic and elaborative literature in order to highlight the importance of moral values and ethical decisions for effective educational leadership. In educational institutes, effective and ethical leadership refers to the implementation of ethical code of conduct in making administrative decisions.

Educational Framework and Ethical Leadership

Haughey (2007) says that there is a direct relation of effective leaders with the educational system and learners. When all these components of an educational system are united together at one platform they constitute the educational framework. This study also points the factor that educational aspects are delicate and therefore the framework is needed to be flexible to deal with every kind of dilemma. This study suggests that there are three components of an effective educational leader. These factors are presence of mind, responsible behavior and authentic ethical knowledge. According to Starratt (2004) moral character of an educational leader reflect hi responsible behavior towards all administrative aspects. An authentic educational leader refers to such a leader which knows his responsibilities in every circumstance and fulfills his duties with in the ethical limitations.

Summary of the Literature Review

The above literature review is based on a number of studies and theories which highlight a number of aspects of effective and ethical leadership, ethical decision making and educational leaders. All of the above discussion and review of literary work reflect the idea that there ethical decision covers all the organizational and individual requirements. Most of the researchers agree that ethical decisions can serve the purpose of implementation of legal code of conduct. The theoretical side of the literature review also elaborated that influence of a number of factors which include initial knowledge about ethics, family, teachers, psychological aspects, social setup and organizational environment, on the decision making process. Theories also focus the factor that approaches of ethical decisions may vary with the personal perspective and insight about ethical values.

The personal point of view of leaders also makes them to analyze the flaws in their perspective, actions, behavior and beliefs in making decisions. Theories suggest that that this experience helps in broadening the vision of leaders about ethics and decisions making. Effectiveness of leadership can be utilized in setting up guidelines for followers to make ethical decisions and follow ethical code of conduct in daily activities. Studies also suggest that there are number of sectors where the capabilities of leaders to make ethical decisions are tested. One of such delicate sectors is economic sector. The literature review also focuses the present organizational trends and their influence on ethical decision making. Theories regarding the influence of integrity, moral intensity and honesty are also being discussed in the literature review. The need of ethical leader cannot be denied in educational institutes. Educational institutes serve as the platform to educate the youth about ethics therefore leadership in education is needed to deliver successful ethical knowledge.

CHAPTER 3: METHODOLOGY

This chapter provides the details of the research methodology adopted for the current study. Further it elucidates the adopted data collection and data analysis techniques to meet the research requirements. The methodological steps followed by the researcher are provided.

Research Design

The methodology used in this research is based on Ethnography Primary Qualitative Research. Focused interview session seemed to be the most appropriate method of all qualitative analysis techniques because it assists in attaining first-hand information from concerned resources (Hancock, 2002). The interview was conducted in a semi structured manner.

Approaches of Qualitative and Quantitative Research

The two most common approaches adopted generally are qualitative and quantitative (Andersonl, 2006). The approaches of these two methods differentiate them from each other and adopt different approaches for addressing the research questions and the problems of the study. The data collection methods and the techniques of analysing and interpreting data are also different. The data evaluation methods are also different from each other for both approaches. The form of data obtained for each of the research methodology is also different. The data for the qualitative research approach are in descriptive form while for the quantitative research approach the data is obtained in the form of numbers and figures (Reisman, Gienapp & Stchowiak, n.d.).

When it comes to realizing the validity of each of the research approaches it could be said that each of the approach is valid in explaining the significant issues and the answers to the research questions (Clarke, 2005). The validity of the research methodology adopted for any research study depends on the application and the execution of the research study. Over the years both of the research methods have proved their credibility in answering the research questions and provided scientific solutions to the issues raised in the research studies. These two approaches are also complementary to one another and when deployed in analyzing one study they could produce better and credible and more reliable results (Patton & Cochran, 2002).

The mixed methodology as the name suggests is the blend of quantitative and the qualitative approaches. This research methodology is applied with multiple strategies. Mixed method research design follows certain steps and phases that involve several strategies to include data comparison and integration in the research design (Creswell, 2005). The mixed method approach makes the findings of the research that is conducted strong and reliable by applying several strategies that follow certain patterns and testing of the hypothesis and verification of the research results.

Another advantage of incorporating mixed method approach is the use of its abduction, which reveals and defines the suitable and reliable account on the results (Onwuegbuzie

& Leech, 2006). This method for methodology is very famous and integrated in many research studies because of the advantages it offers. It is the preference for many researches of the bridge it provides to integrate quantitative and qualitative methods using better clarification in defining and relating the variables of the research (Onwuegbuzie & Leech, 2006).

Restatement of the Purpose of the study

The topic of the study is related to leadership in an organization. The purpose of this study is to discuss the behaviour of leaders' that are linked with the effectiveness of the leadership. The perceptions and the theories regarding the leadership practices and ethical decision making by the leaders and the processes and the ethical guidelines that needs to be followed. The current research paper takes into account the effectiveness of leadership in an educational environment. This research study also discusses the ethical considerations in the ethical decision making process that the leaders follow in their leadership practices.

Research Method Approach

The research methodology is considered to be an important of a research study. The research method approach adopted for this particular study is qualitative primary ethnography methodology. Primary data will be collected through semi structured interviews. Ethnography method for qualitative research allows investigating through formal and informal interview sessions with concerned persons (Hancock, 2002). This methodology will be adopted because it seems to be the best methodology to address the problems and the questions rose in the first chapter. This research was conducted using a qualitative research method because of the nature of the problem and the goals that this study aimed at achieving. Qualitative research is suitable for exploring a fundamental phenomenon (Onwuegbuzie & Leech, 2006; Morse, 2005).

Qualitative ethnograpgy approach offers the solutions of the problems by making an attempt to understand the patterns on which what is occurring and how (Winget, 2005). The data and information that is going to be collected for providing satisfying answers to the readers will be in explanatory form. The data collected, concepts deployed and meanings derived are explanations to provide satisfying explanations (Onwuegbuzie & Leech, 2006).

In the current study data for formulating the literature review and other evidences will be collected from the online resources. The information and data will be collected from the online publishing materials and authenticated websites. Renowned articles and journals will be consulted as they have the potential to provide accurate evidences and information about the topic f the study. The findings and the conclusion of these articles will be incorporated and analyzed in the research and then it will be linked with the findings of the primary research method and data collected by the researcher. However, further research in compiling the documents will be carried out from the Phoenix University Library Online. For more authentic findings, Phoenix University Library Online several other databases such as ProQuest, JSTOR, EBSCOhost will be referred.

McMillan and Schumacher (1997) stated that qualitative research is based upon assumptions that individuals interpret authenticity as iterative. Qualitative research makes use of questions that are open-ended (Morse, 2005). In the current study open-ended and broad questions provide the participants of the study with the opportunity to record their responses in such a manner which will help them to participate and fully share their opinions about the problem of the research. The research question of the current study enables the respondents to provide their understanding regarding the topic and problems of the study (Vivar, 2007). This helps the researcher to include the answers in the respondent's own words. The study will rely on deductive approach, with an emphasis on gaining the insights for the current study from the primary data that will be collected from the interviews. The nature of the information and data collected requires the researcher to interact with the participants.

Validation for Choosing Ethnography Qualitative Methodology

This study and the derivation of results are based on qualitative research method approach. The collection of the data is based on primary resources and the data is collected in order to visualize and answer the identified and targeted research questions (Spradley, 1979). The approach is chosen because interviewing through ethnographic approach allows interacting with participants in an informal and comfortable way. The qualitative sector of this research study is designed in an interpretative manner. The information obtained during the course of the interview session of the selected panel of participants and the results of this survey based research are complied together to determine and identify the importance of ethical decision making, factors influencing the capabilities of leaders in making ethical decisions and observe the importance of effective leadership in educational institutes. It has been clearly mentioned in the literature review that the study aims at covering all aspects of effective ethical decision making particularly in educational institutes, therefore the questions of the survey have also been formed in such a manner so as to cover all aspects of effective ethical leadership and decision making in educational sector. The selection of participants is also made keeping in view the problem statement of the study and to get most realistic and appropriate answers for analyzing different facets of the study.

According to Bloom and Crabtree (2006) effective qualitative methodology of research intends to explore the knowledge about the subject of study and a good ethnographic interview is designed to make optimum use of participants' knowledge. Chapter 1 of the study clearly mentions the purpose and problem statement of the research that is the need of good ethical educational leaders and what are the factors which influence the potential of these leaders to make ethical decisions. In order to gather appropriate information about these aspects, primary resources seemed to be reliable option to conduct the study in an authentic way. According to Creswell (2001) qualitative research allows to conduct research in a realistic way by letting concerned participants answer the queries. In order to sustain the authentication of the study and to make sure that the research does not deviate from its targeted direction, this approach will be adopted.

Another important justification for adopting this qualitative research approach is that it assists in providing direct and concerned information needed to answer the problem statement of the study. Also, this approach provides more opportunities than other approaches to cover social and cultural aspects by maintaining an interactive contact with participants. Qualitative research methodology allows the researcher to enjoy the advantage of answering all ambiguities from a rich and authentic pool on information.

Pros and cons of the Qualitative Research methodology

Every approach is marked with its pros and cons. The appropriate implementation of the chosen methodology in the target direction always ensures optimization of benefits and assists in fulfilling the purpose of the study. Therefore, the pros and cons of the qualitative research methodology based on primary data for conducting the interview are as follows:

Table 1.Pros and cons *Pros and cons*	
Pros	Cons
Offers an easy and realistic way to obtain authentic data.	The reliability of the interview session depends on the skills and potential the interviewer.
Provides first-hand information about the concerned issues.	Interviewer should be capable enough to ask desired questions on the spot if questionnaire does not cover all aspects.
Saves the time of filtering information from previous studies.	Interviewer must have the ability to keep the interviewee in his comfort zone.
Data obtained through primary resources in qualitative methodology is more reliable.	Too much f the information may also cause confusion about keeping and rejecting some pieces of information.
Interview sessions allow validating the collected information through studies.	Interviews may not be able to provide adequate information needed to cover all the aspects of the study.

Assumptions for the chosen methodology

The aim of qualitative research is to understand and observe the importance of the ethical leaderships and influence of ethical decision making on individuals as well as on organizations (Mullane, 2009). The study aims at focusing the cultural, social and psychological influences on the procedure of ethical decision making. There are several key assumptions associated with the quantitative research method which are as follows:

There is a probability of multiple realities but reality is always constructed through social influences. The researcher gets a chance to interact and maintain working relations with other individuals and social groups during the course of completion of and this interaction serves as the primary tool for collecting data collection and carry out analysis. During the course of research the researchers becomes an integral part of the research, and therefore it allows the researcher to understand the value of research and also realize the scenarios with which the concerned people go through. Research is bound to a particular context and all the formulated logics are either based on previous studies or on the information obtained from primary resources. The aim of research is to highlight those theories that assist in explaining the topic of the study.

Research Technique and Process

The research is based on qualitative methodology and all the information collected is from primary resources. The proposed study was conducted through an interview session that aims at covering all the aspects of the research, designed in Chapter 1 of the study. The panels of participants will include10 personnel associated with an educational institute. These members will be interviewed in order to gather information about the influence of ethical leader an ethical decision making on different sectors of the institute.

Sampling Method

According to Creswell (2005) the choice of sampling method is very important and it is also necessary that the chosen sampling method satisfies the needs of the study. It is usually identified before the research is preceded to later stages in order to make sure that the no error is made in analyzing the samples. Sampling has the advantage that it does not waste time and it also ensures the accuracy and precision of data.

There are two sampling methods defined:
1. Purposive Sampling (non-random)
2. Random Sampling

In the present research based study the technique of sampling used will be purposive (non-random) sampling. This technique of sampling is chosen to make sure that experienced, concerned and informed people are consulted for conducting interview because in a purposive sample it is aimed to attain the target of the research for which the study is conducted in the most comprehensive manner that could be possibly implemented to make it definite that the goal of the study is achieved in the end. As it is needed that the influence if ethical leader should be analyzed in different sectors of organizations therefore the members selected for the interview represent a group of leaders belonging to different sectors if the same organization. These officials will also be knowledgeable enough to express their perspective and insight about the area of research.

Instrument Design

The primary instruments which are utilized for conducting this research study will be based on a pre-designed questionnaire for the interview session with the organizational officials. The questions of the interview will be organized in such a manner that it is made sure that a balanced interview was being conducted and every participant is given equal chance to answer interview questions.

Panel Structure

The design of the panel will include 10 members of organizational leaders. The panel will be formed keeping in view the problem statement and research aims and objectives of the study and those people will be consulted for the interview who are capable of delivering required information and satisfactory answers to the interview questions in the opinion of the researcher. As the study deals with the need of educational leader for the promotion of ethical code of conduct therefore those officials will be selected who play the role of decision making in their respective departments.

Data Collection Methods

Two types of data are used in any research study. Primary data is the data that is obtained by the researcher himself and it is then incorporated and interpreted in the analysis section of the research study. The secondary data is the data that is not personally collected by the researcher. Tools for collecting primary and the secondary data are different (Hox & Boeije, 2005). Generally, primary data is collected by the researcher using interviews or the surveys. While on the other hand the secondary data is collected from the previous researches or other secondary sources available out there (Bajpai & Singh, 2009).

Primary Research

To perform this study primary research will be conducted in order to gather reliable and first-hand information on the topic of the research. The research methodology is based in qualitative approach and utilizes the tool of in depth session of interview with the selected members of the organization.

This interview session will be conducted to gather sufficient and essential information about the topic of the study which revolves around the need and influence if an ethical leader. This conducted interview will also assist a great deal in the completion of the study because information gathered will be from those members of the organizations which are directly linked with the decision making process and look through all important administrative matter of the organization. The primary method for the interview seems to be the most appropriate approach in order to address all the aims and objectives of the study. The interview session serves as the primary assisting tool for gathering all desired information.

Data Collection Instruments

Previous Researches

The literature review of the study reflects ideas, perceptions and theories of a number if researchers. The conducted research has utilized a number of previous researches and the insights of other researchers in order to highlight different aspects of the study. These studies are selected keeping in view every possible ambiguity associated with the topic if the study. Online resources play an assistive role in providing access to these literary researches and articles. These articles and studies are chosen for referring to authentic researchers, however the primary tool of research utilized in this study will be the interview session conducted with the concerned members.

Interview session

The study will utilize in depth interview sessions for the collection of primary data in an authentic and reliable manner. The primary data is supposed to be gathered from a collective interview conducted with a panel for 10 members of the organization which play leadership roles in different sectors. Each member of the panel performs delicate duties as a leader and as the study is conducted especially to realize the importance of educational leaders and ethical decision making therefore the panel is formed with thoughtful strategy. As the interview session was going to serve the purpose of the basis of the research therefore the panel formed was able to answer all questions regarding different and complex aspects of the study. The interview session will be open-ended and consist of a carefully designed questionnaire which aims at clarifying all ambiguities of the research. Interview questions will be designed in such a way that participants can reflect their insight regarding the topic under discussion. According to Vivar (2007) in an interview session questionnaire must be designed in such a way that answers given show complete depth about the topic. In this qualitative research studies were also utilized in conducting a complete and detailed research answering all the problem statements mentioned in the study. The capabilities of selected participants were also utilized in a thoughtful way to make the most of the interview session.

Informed Consent

Informed consent is a mandatory part of a research based study. According to B McMillan and Schumacher (1997) informed consent is a significant part of the research and should be integrated in the study as a mandatory inclusion. The informed consent aims at informing the participants about the nature of research and education must be delivered about the significance of the study in informed consent. Notifications about the limits and rules should be clearly mentioned to the participants before beginning the interview session for research. Participants have freedom to make their decision about agreeing to the terms and conditions of the study and should only participate in the interview if there is no objection to any clause of the agreement. There is no space for pressurizing participants to take part in the study against their will (Creswell, 2005; Neuman, 2005).

In the current study, the participants of the interview are informed about the aims and objectives this study had to achieve. Every proper step will be ensured to educate the participants of the combined interview session in order to let them make an informed decision. They are also informed that any of the participants were not forced and they hold the right of withdrawing from the study.

Ethical Limitations

As this study covers the importance of ethical decision making and ethics in leaderships therefore consideration of the ethical issues was very important during the research. During entire interview it will be kept in mind that, that no particular religion is targeted or quoted while discussing the importance and influence of spiritual beliefs on ethical values. The panel which will participate in the interview also pointed that disclosing any confidential information about the organization was considered as the violation of the organizational policy. Moreover, the rules and regulations of the organizational environment where the interview is going to be held will be followed strictly. Keeping in view the delicacy of the profession interviewees will not be kept engaged for a long time in order to fulfill the ethical obligation about saving the time and energy of interviewees which can be served in educating and building ethical values of students. While proposing questions about the ethical code of conduct, no organizational department will be targeted in particular. Questions will be designed in order to gather maximum information about the perception of organizational leaders about the importance of ethical influence on the effectiveness of the leadership.

CHAPTER 4:
ANALYSIS AND DISCUSSION

Chapter 4 provides details of the actual work done in this research study. To satisfy the research aims and objectives and simultaneously answer the research questions of this study Ethnography Primary Qualitative Research methodology was adopted. Interview sessions were held and a panel of 10 participants appeared in the session. A total of eleven questions were asked from each participant. Keeping the ethical considerations in mind before commencing the interview the participants were briefed about the purpose of the study and the statement of the problem as an effort to urge them for participating sincerely in the interview and be a part of making the leadership practices effective for the future leaders.

Moreover, the researcher carried out a theoretical analysis of the interview responses obtained from the participants and no analysis software like NVivo was used. Furthermore, the research was completely based on interview analysis hence, this study is marked as a qualitative study and no triangulation of data is required.

Demographic Analysis

To investigate the research questions of the current study 10 participants were interviewed. The demographic attributes and its graphical representation of the selected participants are provided below:

Gender of the Participants:

Gender

Table 2. Gender				
	Frequency	Percent	Valid Percent	Cumulative Percent
Male	7	70.0	70.0	70.0
Female	3	30.0	30.0	100.0
Total	10	100.0	100.0	

The above table shows that out of 10 participants of the interview session, 7 were male and 3 were female. Below pie diagram shows the graphical representation of the interview participants.

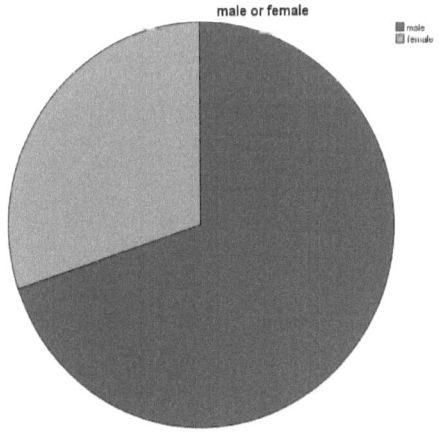

Figure 1. **Gender**

Race/ ethnicity of the Participants

Race/Ethnicity

Table 3. *Race/Ethnicity*				
	Frequency	Percent	Valid Percent	Cumulative Percent
White	4	40.0	40.0	40.0
Black or African	3	30.0	30.0	70.0
Asian	1	10.0	10.0	80.0
Others	2	20.0	20.0	100.0
Total	10	100.0	100.0	

The above table shows that majority of the participants that is 4 were white. 3 were black, 1 was Asian and rest belonged to other ethnic groups.

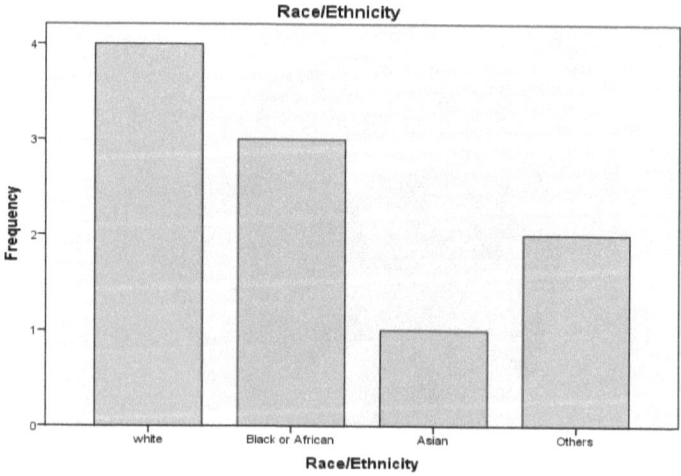

*Figure 2.***Race/Ethnicity**

Age Group of participants

Age Group

Table 4. Age Group	Frequency	Percent	Valid Percent	Cumulative Percent
26-30 years	1	10.0	10.0	10.0
31-35 years	4	40.0	40.0	50.0
Above 35	5	50.0	50.0	100.0
Total	10	100.0	100.0	

The table above reveals that majority of the participants were aged above 35 years which means that the interview panel consisted of experienced and professional personnel therefore the responses acquired from them would be reliable and realistic.

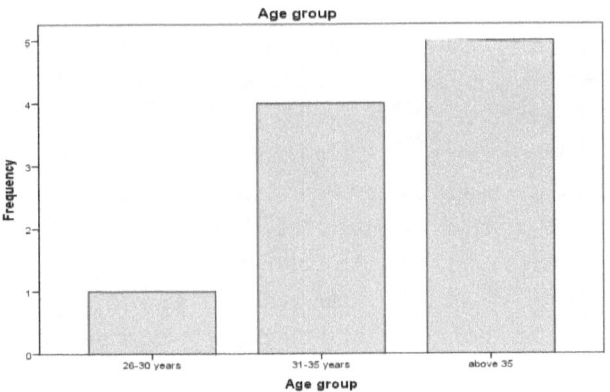

Figure 3. **Age Group**

Interview Analysis

During the interview session a total of twelve Questions were asked, responses were gathered from the interviewees and then analyzed. Following is the interview analysis for the current research study.

1) How do you define leadership?

This question was posed to the panel in order to gain the basic idea of leadership. Though everyone as a response to this interview gave his/he own definition of leadership yet the responses of each of the participants nearly the same to this question. One of the respondents said, "I believe leadership is an art. It helps in acquiring those results that can only be achieved through working together in the form of a group with the same purpose and destiny in mind". Another respondent declared, "Leadership, in my opinion is an act of providing a group of people with information, and knowledge regarding something. Leadership is supposed to create a vision of some task and it also defines the methods of achieving that task in order to achieve the targeted goals." On more of the respondents gave a different perspective for defining leadership in the following words, "I define leadership as a process during which a group of people tries to achieve some independent as well as mutual targets and the real process of leadership helps them in doing so by help them eliminating the issues and the concerns in doing so." Another valuable definition for leadership was contributed by a respondent in the following words, "I consider leadership as a science as the leader is supposed to carry out a task with the help of team members by devising favorable situations for creating a new substance at the end of the process." All the participants reacted to this question in their own way and came up with new and different aspects of defining leadership. As the interview panel constituted of people linked with the practices of leadership therefore, their responses to this question was necessary and helpful in formulating the preamble for the analysis and the discussion part of the study.

2) What is the real characteristic of a good leader?

The second question was directed to the participants was to extract what their opinion is about the characteristics of an effective and a good leader. A respondent indicated that the real characteristic of a good leader is his/her self awareness. He further elaborated if a person is able to deal with the strengths and the weaknesses of his/her own personality that would help in organizing things in the best possible manner in a timely fashion and then he can be a good leader and would be able to push his followers to their better potential by understanding their demands and requirements. Another participant defined the real characteristic of a leader in the following words, "Selflessness is the real quality of a good leader. A good leader is one who does not work only for his personal gains but for brining a positive change in the society and in the life of others through his vision and goals he formulates in the light of that vision." The answer of another respondent brought into light another very important characteristic that a leader should possess in order to be good and that was ability to motivate his/her team members. He further elaborated his statement by adding that a good leader does not tell others what they have to do rather he inspires them and motivates them by creating some sense of satisfaction about the task that they together are supposed to achieve. Responses of other participants highlighted other characteristics of a good leader such as ability to deal with tough situations with calmness and not create panic, creativity of ideas for achieving certain tasks and goals, wisdom and practicality in implementation solutions and demanding work to be done by the team members.

3) Which forms of leadership are associated with educational effectiveness?

The respondents were asked to shed light over the forms of leadership that can be adopted for being an effective educational leader. Not much difference was observed in their responses. Most of the respondents declared their opinion that transformational form of leaderships is the most associated and appropriate type connected with the educational effectiveness. One of the respondents quoted the following reason so as to why transformational form of leadership was suitable for educational effectiveness, "As the educational programs and the educational system is always reforming and re-structured, so transformational type of leadership fits best within educational effectiveness". Another participant linked the fact that since the vision of educational leaders is to bring positive change in the society, therefore this form enables them to communicate their vision in an appropriate manner and it lets them be aware of the benefits they together are to achieve by creating a sense of responsibility among all. In three of the respondents opinion along with the transformational form of leadership, instructional form of leadership is also important to be incorporated for educational effectiveness. As replied by one respondent, "For educational effectiveness transformational as well as instructional forms of leaderships are significant, as both of these forms help in improving the delivery of vision and scope of the task the team is working on and the leaders is guiding them." The key of transformational leadership is the involvement of all the members of the team on one platform that lets everyone to make contribution in improvement of the system and coupled with it the instructional form of leadership enables the administration to bring about the techniques of improvement by analyzing the weak areas and develop standard solutions for improving the system.

4) What is the importance of ethics in decision-making in organizations?

To cover the basics of the topic the fourth question was asked to the participants to contribute their opinion about the importance of ethics in decision making process in organizations. Valuable responses were received from the participants. One of the respondents said ethics hold great importance in every walk of life. He further added with relevance to the question particularly in an organization the process of decision making becomes crucial as the interests of stakeholders and the society needs to be taken into strict consideration as well. Another respondent added, "in organizations it is very significant to consider ethics because the mission or the task carried out by any organization is to ultimately impact the society and therefore, every decision is to be taken with such care that interests of all employees and other staff is protected so that they remain dedicated to the mission of the organization so that it brings positive change in the society." One senior respondent opined in the following words, "Being a part of a mission oriented organization makes it even more critical for the decision makers to hold firmly the ethical guideline as there should not be any sign of biasness during the decision making." Next respondent seconded this statement by adding that biasness if not taken care of while decision making impacts the effectiveness and productivity of employees and few of them feel themselves undervalued. The statement of the last respondent is necessary to be mentioned here as it concluded the responses of all the participants, "Concluding it all, ethical decisions in the light of proper code of ethics should be made in an organization as this will automatically safeguard the interests of everyone. As in organizations delicate decisions need to be made that regarding significant issues that involve employees and in some cases even their families, so it is necessary that ethical approach is adopted while decision making process."

5) What are the psychological and the social aspects that can endanger individuals' principles?

The question was formulated in order to analyze how social and psychological aspects impact one's principles and moral values. This question received diversified reviews from participants. One of the participants answered, "The collective values followed by a society ultimately affect individual's principles. Those principles cannot be practiced by an individual which are hindered by social barriers". Talking about psychological aspects, a participant answered, "Social and domestic background decided always influence a person psychologically. A person with stable domestic background will have firmly formed moral values and principles as compare to the person who is psychologically disturbed". Another participant shared opinion as, "Society and home are the first influences on a human mind. They decide the psychological stability and ultimately formation of principles". From the perspective of leadership and ethical decision making, the question aimed at identifying those social and psychological aspects which have the potential of endangering individual's principles. Specifying a few of those aspects, a participant said, "The wave of global crisis has hit every society on equal level, but those societies which were already unstable have gone from worse to worst. The financial crisis has given rise to a number of circumstances which are forcing individuals to give upon their principles". One of the participants said, "Early childhood years affect the psychology of a person in the most influential way. Early hardships impact a person psychologically and such a person does not have strongly formed principles". From the analysis of participants' responses it is concluded the collective moral values of a society and domestic background are two of the many factors which can endanger individual's principles. Most of the participants agreed that a financially unstable society has a great potential to force individuals for adopting unethical principles which certainly impacts effective leadership.

6) Describe your leadership traits in relation with integrity, honesty, and trustworthiness?

This question was posed to the participants in order to determine their views about the importance of integrity, honesty, and trustworthiness by gauging how they incorporate these values in their leadership practices. One participant declared, "I believe in religion and all my life activities are guided by religion. So in leadership, as well the religious values stay ahead of me and honesty is the most highlighted trait of my leadership practices. My every decision and the activity in leadership take into account the principles of honesty and sincerity with my profession and colleagues." Another respondent stated honesty as his leadership traits in the following words, "I believe in fairness and one can only be fair in his leadership practices if he embraces truthfulness and honesty in his leadership practices." One respondent reflected, "Trustworthiness would best describe my leadership trait. I said so because I never make any decision with a high hand. I believe in open door policy and if my followers put their trust in me then and only then I would be an influential and effective leader." The responses of majority of the participants declared honesty and integrity as the basic values that guide the practices of contemporary leaders. They were of the opinion that a true and honest leader can be an effective one. One respondent stated, "I am a true believer of the fact that an effective leader is one who builds trust within his team members and that can only be achieved through being honest and sincere. I try best to be honest and that develops trustworthiness itself."

7) What in your opinion helps in dealing with ethical dilemmas during ethical decision making process?

This question was included in the interview questions because the ethical dilemmas in any workplace are common to occur. When this question was directed to the participants it was assumed that they all were aware of the complexity of the situation that an ethical dilemma poses. As a response on participant stated, "during ethical decision making process ethical dilemmas are common to be faced by us. In my opinion a systematic approach that considers all the aspects in detail helps in dealing with such complex situations." Another respondent said, "I believe in a bottom up approach for dealing with an ethical dilemma. By bottom up approach I mean that the decision maker considers the final and the most favourable result of the situation and then consider the action to be taken accordingly." Another respondent viewed this question in somewhat different perspective and provided the researcher with the following answer, "I consider an informal meeting with the potential stakeholders of the situation helps in dealing with the complexities of and ethical decision making process of the ethical decision making process. The involvement of sensible and sincere team members in dealing with the situation helps the leader to make an effective and sound decision to solve the quandary an ethical dilemma causes." Two respondents reflected, the ethical guidelines and the code of ethics that are followed in their educational settings help them taking decision when faced with an ethical quandary. Few of the participants even acknowledged peers, former experiences, and their own observations to help them with ethical dilemma. Another participant suggested that the values of an individual leader can also help in guiding him through such a situation.

8) What are the factors that affect your ethical decision making process?

Through this question the researcher aimed at enquiring of the participants about the elements that influence their ethical decisions. All the respondents contributed eagerly to let the researcher know about what actually affects them while taking any major ethical decision. One of the respondents said, "As I mentioned earlier, I come from a religious family. All my life dealings and activities exhibit my religious values, therefore, I believe that my religious values do influence the decisions that I make." Another respondent reflected that his personal values and principles affect the ethical decisions that he takes. Moving on to the next participants with the same question it revealed that principles values and principles top the list among the factors that affect the decisions and choices they make during their leadership. One more respondent stated, "Besides any other factor, environment influences my ethical decision making of ethical dilemmas. The environment in which the ethical issue arise influences the solution as well. Along with this the mission of the organization I work in also produces its effects on my decision." It was shared by another respondent that the impact of the problem and its impact on the society do make a difference to the decisions that he make. Some respondents declared that the way decisions and the issue is going to affect the stakeholders of the organizations also affect their ethical decision making process. Another respondent reflected values and the set of morals she believes in do not fail in affecting her decisions. Concluding it, certain factors and elements that can affect the decision making of a leader surfaced through the responses received

Sam Eldakak

from the participants. These factors were personal morals and religious values, interests of the stakeholders, vision of the organization and impact on society influence the ethical decisions of the participant leaders.

9) How your personal values affect your decision making process?

The participants were asked this question in order to gain the insights of their traits of leaderships and how they actually take the decisions. One respondent stated, "Well, I am kind of a result oriented person and whenever I take any decision I keep in mind the final consequences of that decision." Another respondent reflected his desire to bring a positive change in the society and further elaborated the decisions he make he keeps in mind the consequences and impacts of that decision on the society. They try to figure out such solutions to the problems that affect the society in a positive manner. In general, this is an important trait of a leader that he tries his best that the decision he takes do not impact any one, society in general in any adverse manner. Another participant mentioned that he never takes any decision without the consent of his team members because he thinks that decision things with such approach de-motivate the members and the vision and the mission that the share is affected because this would not encourage them to give their best to the project they are working together. This is his approach because it is his values to respect others and their opinions. One respondent said, "I am a true believer that experiences are your best teacher. So, I try to incorporate the lessons I get from my past or even others experiences to guide me through the ethical decision making process." This question was very important as this reflected the insights of the educational and ethical leaders that how their personal values could affect the decisions that they make in an environment. Respect for others, sensitivity

64

to the society and personal traits of a person are likely to affect the decisions that they make.

10) What sort of difficulties do you experience during an ethical decision making process?

The participants were asked to reflect on this question because their answers to this question would help the researcher to know in general the difficulties of the leaders they face during their leaderships practices while making an ethical decision. One participant opined, "this sometimes becomes difficult to express the importance of a matter to the team members and keep them motivated. As soon as a problem arises and those who are less focussed or something gets panic and then it is a big challenge to keep them calm, motivated and focussed along with devising a solution to the problem." Another participant said, "if a problem arises between the employees relating to their adjustments with each other is a challenge. As along with the targeted project and its issues team building is sometimes challenging and keep the participants all together and dedicated to each other becomes at times difficult." Another respondent stated, "It becomes very difficult for me to make a decision without getting over influenced by my personal values. Sometimes the problems that occur are of such sorts that makes it difficult for me not to consider the extremes of my personal values and it becomes defying task to find a solution that satisfies and balances the personal as well the organizational and the leadership values." This satisfying of the personal values as well the organizational values was also quoted by few of the other members of the interviewee panel. Similarly, other respondents also declared that to keep the mission and the vision of the organizations on the line and ahead of all else becomes difficult during an ethical dilemma.

11) What piece of advice would you give to future leaders to be an effective leader?

This was a very significant question to be asked from the participants as they all were well experienced and senior in their organizations. One of the respondents said, "I would suggest the future leaders to be consistent and true to them. If they would be true and honest to themselves they would automatically guard their decision and practices to be so." Another respondent suggested, "Think and think thoroughly before deciding on something. Evaluate the consequences of your action and decisions then you can be able to an effective and inspirational leader". One more respondent stated, "As to one of your questions I supported the cause of trust building. I would like to suggest the same to the future leaders to build trust within the team and organization because you are the leader as you team will follow you and for that you have to be a trustworthy person in order to attract and motivate your team." Another participant quoted her suggestion in the following words, "Work on yourself a lot. By work I mean keep managing your actions according to the situation. Always remember that you have to lead and people are relying on your capabilities. This will give you a sense of responsibility and will guide you with your leadership practices." Other participants also made some similar but valuable suggestions that the future leaders should believe in themselves and build confidence in their actions. It was also suggested from one of the participant that they should think good for others and good will happen with them. IT was also recommended that the future leaders take ethical training sessions to seek help during their leadership practices. The gist of suggestions from few of the participants is that future leaders should try to depict honesty and integrity in their actions and this would automatically guide them to the path of glory of being an effective leader.

Discussion on the Interview Question Responses

The careful selection of interview questions aimed at an extensive evaluation of participants' reviews regarding the importance of ethical decision making and effective leadership. The interview began with the definition of leadership to get an idea about the insight of participants about the topic. As the interview panel constituted of participants who are rendering services as leaders at different levels and in different departments, therefore their reviews about this question were very important to conduct further discussion. Although every participant revealed their opinion differently yet their approach was somewhat similar. All the participants mutually agreed that leadership is a very delicate responsibility and the effectiveness of leadership is ultimately judged by the nature of influence on those who are led.

When asked about characteristics of a good leader, each participant responded in a different manner. The question was formed to analyze that which qualities are prioritized to be a good leader. The quality of a leader to motivate his team members was marked as one of the most important qualities of a good leader by all the participants. Another characteristic highlighted by many of the participants is the ability of a leader to cope with circumstances within ethical limits. According to responses, a good leader must be capable of dealing with all kinds of situations by following ethical code of conduct and has the tendency to aqcuire their aspiration. Participants were asked which form of leadership should be adopted by leaders for educational effectiveness. The responses received did not differ vastly and most of the participants agreed that transformational form of leadership is the most appropriate form which can be adopted for effective leadership in educational limits. Participants said that coordination and mutual planning is very important particularly in mission oriented organizations. Therefore, the above analysis concludes transformational leadership can motivate the members to work in a collaborative environment. Moreover, transformational form of leadership also helps the leaders and the task force to achieve the aspirations.

The question about importance of ethics in decision making process particularly in organizations aimed at forming the ground of the discussion of the study. Analyzing the received responses it can be concluded, ethical decision making can make the leadership effective for influencing the members of the organization to work in accordance with the ethical code of conduct. Responses also highlighted the fact that ethical leader motivates his team members to follow his footsteps which ultimately helps in maintaining a collaborative working environment. This even helps in attaining the goals of the organization in collaborative and inspirational environment.

Participants also highlighted a number of social and psychological factors which influence the ethical decision making of a leader. Participants agreed that the social setup and values presiding in a society influence the principles and values of a person. A crisis stricken society does not have much potential to produce leaders with firmly formed ethical values. The analysis also concludes that early childhood years have the greatest influence on the psychology of a person. Ethical beliefs are formed in young age and then social circumstances decide the strength of these beliefs. Participants declared integrity, honesty and trustworthiness as three basic pillars for being an ethical and effective leader.

Keeping in view the probability of ethically challenging situations in a workplace, the responses of participants in this regard were of prime importance. Participants came up with different responses. Analysis of these responses concludes the fact that setting priorities is the most important tool in coping with such situations. Respondents said that strategic planning and clear knowledge about ethical decision making are two key factors which can help a leader to make ethical decisions, even in challenging situations. Participants were asked to advise future leaders and they considered for effective leaderships and ethical decision making, understanding the importance of honesty and sincerity is very important.

Link between Research aims and objectves and the findings

The interview questions were formulated before approaching the participants for interview sessions. These were formulated by keeping in the research aims, objectves, and the resaerch questions. The interview questions 1, 2 and 3 aimed at exploring the characteristics of a good leader. The participants' responses helped in achieving this aim. Unselfish behaviour, ability to motivate and many others were considered as good qualities of the leders as per the participants responses.

Interview question 3 explored the forms of leadership that are associated with educational effectiveness. As per the responses the transformational and instructional leaderships remained most highlighted according to the findings of the study. Inteview questions 8, 9, and 10 tried to identify the difficulties faced by leaders during ethical decision making. According to the responses the protection of personal values, religious values, protection of organizational values and satisfcation of employees pose great difficulties in ethical decision making.

Interview question 5 aimed at divulging the psychological and the social aspects that can endanger individual principals. According to the reponses Social and domestic background, childhood years affect the psychology of a person are likely to affect the psychology of a person.

Themes Developed from the Interview Responses and their Analysis

The themes deducedd from the anaalysis section are formulated in the table below:

Table 5: *Deduced Themes from Analysis*		
Themes	Interview Questions	Participants Responses
Good leaders are selfless and inspiring	Question 1 and 2	Participants responded that those who are selfless and consider organizational benefits above their personal benefits are good leaders. Moreover, those who have the ability to inspire their followers prove to be good and effective leaders.
Transformational form of leadership is associated with educational effectiveness	Question 3	According to findings the transformational leadership is best suited as it takes into consideration the opinions of all the team members in order to bring change in the system. Moreover it helps in analyzing the conflict of interests among the employees and decision is taken accordingly.

Ethical decision making is very critical for an organization	Question 4	Decision making in an organization should be ethical and according to the proper cope of ethics as it will automatically safeguard the interests of the organization and its stakeholders.
Leadership traits of a leader are reated to integrity, honesty, and trustworthiness	Question 6,11	Effective leaders are honest and develop a certain level of trustworthiness with their followers
Personal values affect the process of ethical decision making	Question 6, 7, 8 and 9	During an ethical dilemma in an organization satisfying the personal values and the organizational values is difficult yet necessary.

Summary

This section of the chapter's states the summary of above four chapter of the topic called "Educational and Ethical Leadership—Best Practice". The first chapter of this provided the details of the background and the scope that this study holds within. The objective of this research was to gain essential knowledge about the practices of the educational and ethical leadership in an organization during ethical decision making. An extensive review of the literature covering maximum aspects of leadership was provided. A theoretical framework was developed and ethical decision making in leadership was reviewed. Theories for ethical decision making along with educational leadership practices were discussed. The aims and objectives were achieved using the qualitative primary data collection methods i.e. interviews. Semi-structured interview session was conducted with the panel using 11 pre-formulated relevant questions. All the ethical considerations were taken care of the by researcher before, during and after the data collection technique. For primary data, the researcher approached 10 participants via proper agreement through consent form where no participant has been forced for any contribution. The participation of each selected participant is voluntary. Their responses were theoretically analysed and themes were formulated from the questions asked to them and their received responses. The next sessions will be concluding the findings of this study in a comprehensive manner and then they will be narrowed down to answer the research questions of the study. Recommendations will also be provided in the light of the findings of the research.

CHAPTER 5:
CONCLUSION AND RECOMMENDATIONS

The final chapter of the current study provides the concluding statements covering all the aspects covered in during the research. Then in the light of the concluding remarks few recommendations have been put forward by the researcher. The first chapter of this provided the details of the background and the scope that this study holds within. This has been realized that the final success of an organization lies in the abilities of the leaders leading the mission of the organization. This is so because they are the people leading the employees and keeping them on track for achieving the targets and the mission of the organization. It is the leader and his potential abilities that develops and provides clear vision to his followers through his leadership skills. Since a long time leaders and their leadership traits and skills have been of significant concern to the researchers and many studies have taken into consideration the task of determining the key association of leaders and their traits and skills of leadership to the success of the organization they are associated with. Therefore, it was intended through the study at hand to ascertain how leaders through their effective leadership set the basis for ethical compliance which works as a catalyst for organizations to respect ethnicity as a core value set. The objective of this research was to gain indispensable knowledge regarding the aspects of educational and ethical leadership. Themes have been developed by the researcher according to the interview questions and the received responses of the participants. These deduced themes fulfil the requirements of the study and states some facts related to best practice regarding educational and ethical leadership. Moreover, these derived themes also state facts related to ethical decision making process during leadership.

Restatement of Research Questions

Research question formation is one of the most important and basic task accomplished before commencing the research study. These questions work as a guiding tool for the researcher and help in determining and aligning the key findings for the study. Same approach as adopted by the research while designing the research questions for the current dissertation. It was taken care that the research questions cover the basics to cover in this research study. Following four research questions were formulated keeping in view the research scope and problem statement of the study.

1) What is the real characteristic of a good leader?
2) Which forms of leadership are associated with educational effectiveness?
3) What are the difficulties faced by leaders during ethical decision making?
4) What are the psychological and the social aspects that can endanger individual principals?

Research Methodology Adoption

The research questions and the objectives designed to be covered in this study helped in determining the research methodology to be adopted for satisfying the readers with the content of the research. For collecting data and information to be analysed and discussed in the current study Qualitative methodology was selected as this would help the researcher in exploring in detail the information and ideas shared by the participants. This was important for the researcher to understand and gauge the scope and the significance of their responses. In particular Ethnography Primary Qualitative Research methodology was adopted. Focused interview session was carried out by the researcher that involved each and every participant consulted for the course of the study. This method proved to be the most appropriate one of all qualitative analysis techniques because it assisted in acquiring firsthand knowledge and information from concerned resources (Hancock, 2002). For the deriving conclusions and formulating recommendations in this qualitative study a detailed data analysis of the responses of participants to the interview questions was used so the researcher could determine the key words and information that participants revealed as being potentially significant in contributing to the facts achieved and comprehended from the research. The researcher approached the participants along with a pre set questionnaire provided in the appendix of this document. The formulation of the interview questions was very crucial as the whole analysis and the later sections of the study depended on it.

The researcher designed the questions keeping in view the basics of the research study as described in chapter 1. The interview questions aimed at covering the basics of the research questions and research objectives as well as the underlying principles kept in mind while constructing the interview questions. Each decided interview question was important in the development of the findings of the research study and covered the standards of educational and ethical leadership practices. This qualitative study helped in integrating the perceptions and opinions of the participants to address the gaps in the leadership practices of the modern leaders.

Interview session was held and a panel of 10 participants appeared in the session. A total of eleven questions were asked from each participant. The participants were approached after they agreed to the informed consent that described them the problem statement and urged them to be a part of this study. Then before the interview session the ethical considerations were also kept in mind. Keeping the ethical considerations in mind before commencing the interview the participants were again briefed about the purpose of the study and the statement of the problem as an effort to reveal the importance of the study and their participation. This even encouraged them for participating genuinely in the interview and be a part of making the leadership practices effective for the future leaders.

Conclusion

The research studies that have been conducted in the name of leadership covers the discipline of leaderships by finding out the nature of leadership qualities of a triumphant and experienced leader. The researcher did not encounter any significant and noteworthy research study that explored the issues in the ethical decision making process faced by the contemporary leaders. The process of ethical decision making is critical in the mission and vision oriented organizations (Christensen & Kohls, 2003). As it doubles the responsibilities of the leaders to adopt a balanced, systematic and strategic approach to take decision that involve ethical concerns. The protection of interests of the individuals and the organization as well should be the top priority of the leaders in such cases (Boal & Hooijberg, 2000).

Interview questions 1, 2, 3, 5, and 6 of the interview session aimed at covering the basics of the leaderships and traits of the leaders. The participants considered leaderships and art, science or a process. Each justified his and her definition in a definable manner. According to the discussion the basic fruit to be obtained as a result of leaderships is the completion of the task the leaders and his followers are appointed to accomplish in the best possible and the ethical manner. It is the duty of the leader to provide guidance to his followers to make a task possible to occur. Leadership is a process or a method that creates vision for the others and the employees within the organization which helps them in attaining the defined and the pre-set goals of the organization. The responses of the participants make it important to mention here that the course of effective leadership should be such that it adopts a balanced approach towards attaining the goals of the organization as well as the individual targets to be achieved. A new concept was put forward by a participant who viewed leadership as a science. He justified his response very well by stating that the followers and their resources are ingredients or substance and the leaders are the catalyst or the gearing force that alters the rate of task accomplishment through their ethical and education effectiveness, producing entirely new substance as a result of the process. This concludes that although the definition of the leaders for describing their profession may acquire different forms of words and ways but the essence is the same that it is the leaders that hold the greatest responsibility of making something true out of the capabilities of his followers and employees. This also made clear that the leads of the modern world do feel the seriousness and importance of their profession to the individuals whom they are leading and to the organizations they belong to. For achieving this purpose it is necessary for the leaders to posses some of the real characteristics that distinguish them from all other ordinary people. As said by Avolio and Gardener (2005), the leader leads and the manager does. This makes the responsibility and task of the leader more important and crucial because the effectiveness of the final results depends on his capabilities and qualities of leading (Bennis, 2000).

Integrity, honesty and trustworthiness are considered as three basic pillars or qualities of an ethical and effective leader. Acording to the findings it can easily be concluded that the these qualities in a leader introduces transparency in his dealings with his employees and this also encourages the followers to be dedicated to their tasks and work. The data analysis concludes that the religious leaders are bound to be honest as honesty is the ritual of every religion being practiced on earth. The decision and the activities of such leaders take into consideration the principles of honesty and sincerity with their profession and the employees working under them. Many different responses about the qualities and traits of leadership from the participants were observed as a result of an interview question. According to the discussion based on the interview analysis helps in concluding that honesty is also one of the necessary qualities possessed by ethical leaders. If a leader is honest, he would be fair in his dealings and would become the role model for the followers following his directions and he would be able to motivate them towards achieving the set targets. Team building is also one of the qualities that is important for the leaders in order to be effective in their practices (Hallinger, 2003). A leader would only be able to build a team if he has certain qualities that involve building trust among the employees and his followers. Trustworthiness also came to the surface as an important quality for ethical and educational leaders. Open door policy encourages the followers to put their trust in their leader which ultimately makes the leader influential and effective by holding up the mark of being trustworthy

(Clawson, 2006). This discussion concludes that an effective leader is one who builds trust within his team members and that can only be achieved through being honest and sincere. All in all, it could be said that the effective leader is able to motivate his followers through his fair dealings and he would be fair in his dealings if he is honest and sincere to his profession. An honest and loyal leader would be selfless and would gain the trust of his fellowmen naturally without any effort. All these will ultimately affect the productivity of the organization and their aims would be achieved (Bolman & Deal, 2003).

The interview question two aimed at acquiring the knowledge of the characteristics that an ethically and educationally effective leader should posses. The discussion helps in concluding a number of real and genuine qualities of a leader. The most important characteristic that a leader should posses is the ability to motivate and guide his followers. All other qualities of the leaders are the sub parts of this quality. As indicated self awareness of the leaders is one of the real characteristics that leader should have to be effective leaders because if he is capable of evaluating himself and his employees with same scale then he would be able to motivate and guide them. The quality of selflessness is also a sub quality because only that leader would be able to motivate and inspire his followers who are transparent in his dealings in the eyes of his team members. If a leaders does not hold posses this quality and exhibits corrupt and unethical behavior by making such decisions that cover only his interest would never be able to stir the urge of accomplishing any task in his team members. Other sub qualities as suggested in the study were ability to deal with tough and critical situations with calmness and not create panic, devising innovative ideas for achieving defined tasks and objectives, wisdom and practicality for implementation of solutions. All these characteristics would automatically be possessed by the leaders who inspires and motivates his followers to follow his directions and guidelines. Or in other words, the leader who posses these qualities would automatically become a motivational, effective and an ideal leader to lead a task force. As supported by Sankar (2003) such a leader would not have to tell his members about what they have to do rather he would inspire and motivate them by establishing a sense of satisfaction about being a part of the task that they together would achieve under his dynamic and transparent leadership. Effective leader is one who works in an organized and timely manner to achieve the tasks along with his followers. This also lies within the abilities of a leader to push his followers to their best potential by utilizing their individual skills and qualities by being considerate about their demands and requirements.

The discussion and analysis of the participants' responses revealed that transformational leadership form is best associated with educational effectiveness. This is so because the vision of the educational leaders of bringing positive change in the society, makes transformational form of leadership to be best suited for the educational leaders. This fact would help them in communicating their vision with the other members of the organization in proper manner and it would help them be aware of the advantages and benefits they together would achieve as being a team by creating a sense of responsibility among the team members (Avolio & Yammarino, 2002). Moreover, any conflict in interest arising among the emplyees awould be settled on the spot and a mutually agreed decision would be taken. However, few characteristics of instructional forms of leaderships are also significant along with transformational form. This is so because it would help the educational leader in improving their way of deliverance of scope and aims of the task his team is working on under his leadership. Transformational form of leadership provides the chance to the members of the organization to deliver their feedback on the organizational system and together with it the instructional form of leadership would enable the administration to bring into action the techniques for bringing improvement after analyzing the weakness of the areas to develop standard solutions for enhancing the system (Friedman & Langbert, 2000). The transformational form of leaderships brings all the team members and the leaders on one common platform to encourage them in putting forward their ideas and techniques for improvement.

Through the responses of the participants it was observed that the personal principles of a person influence his dealings and similar concept was provided in the study of Waggoner (2010). And it is also important fact that the principles and values of an individual may be altered as a result of the psychological and the social aspects. Therefore, a question was posed to the participants about the psychological and the social aspects that can endanger principles of individuals. It was concluded that the individual principles need to be in accordance with the cultural values of the particular society otherwise they cannot be practiced openly and without criticism. The cultural aspect of the region a person belongs to guides his basic morals and values. The personal values of a person are definitely influenced by their psychological state of mind. A person coming from a stable background will have firm moral values and principles rather than a psychologically disturbed person. The environment that person receives at his first school which is his home of course helps in making up the future morals and values that he will be practicing. In context of ethical decision making in leadership, the social and psychological aspects with the potential of endangering individual's principles are significant because inevitably the personal values of a person do get reflected in his leadership practices (Brown & Trevino, 2006). The impacts of childhood years on the psychology of a person are undeniable. From the discussion it is concluded that values of a society and domestic background endanger individual's principles in the most influential way. A financially unstable society would have greater chances to have morally unstable leaders with unethical values which certainly would affect their leadership traits and practices (Heifetz &Linsky, 2004).

Interview question 4, 7, 8, 9, 10, and 11 covered the most critical issue for the leaders of ethical decision making. As known and observed the leaders are of great importance for any organization because the keep the employees focused and guides them towards best practices. Along with this their task is not only finished here, but to solve the issues within an organization during any situation is also their one of their crucial responsibilities. If an issue that involves ethical quandaries, it becomes even more so important and critical for them to decide upon something that keeps everything smooth and on-going for the organization as well as the employees (Satterlee, 2009). This research study concludes that grip to ethical values and principles are very important for the leaders to be effective within their organizations. If leader fails in establishing a collaborative relation with employees within the formal ethical limits then it would become difficult for him to deliver the targeted objectives and profits to an organization's stakeholders and society. The profit oriented approach may tend the policy makers to overlook the importance of ethical and educational leadership, so in such situations to avoid ethical challenges it becomes difficult for the leaders to be effective and the same theory was suggested by Fulmer (2004). The importance of ethics should be realized by every leader to play their role remarkably. The responsibilities of a leader are to make sure that the ethical decisions that they undertake do not deny anyone's rights and keep the mission of the organization ahead within the framework of the ethical code (Burns, 2004).

The importance of ethics cannot be neglected in the daily dealings. In an organizational setting it is ethically important for the leaders to hold on to the principles of ethics and make the decisions concerning the ethical issues. During any ethical decision making process it should be the priority of a leader to take balanced decisions that safeguard the interest of the stakeholders associated with the organizations and the society of which they all are a part of (Lee &Chang, 2006). It is also the duty of the organizations that they formulate certain code of ethics that cover their mission and guides the leaders through the ethical decision making process so that the decisions that they make do not harm the societal values. The ethical decision making is crucial for the leaders as the decision that they undertake should bring positive change within the settings of the society. The leaders can only be effective and inspirational in true sense if they exhibit fairness through their dealings and therefore, it is important for them to avoid biasness and keep judging their decisions and evaluating their performance with the ethical guidelines. Being not carried away by the ethical dilemma and keep the hold of sanity is difficult for the leaders in critical situations. From the participants systematic approach to be followed was suggested. Day and Shoemaker (2006) also approved of the fact that systematic approach would enable the leaders to review all the specifications of the problem in detail before taking any major ethical decision.

Another bottom up approach was opined by a participant that considers the final consequences and appropriate results of the ethical dilemma and then considers the pros and cons of each one of them and then selects the best one. Calling meetings can also be one of the approaches that could be followed by the leaders to decide upon an ethical decision.

This is a sensible approach as this would involve the feedback from all the stakeholders and each one of them would be able to understand the potential harms and complexities of the situation and this would b somewhat release the burden of the leader, but it is important that the final decision lies within the powers of the leader. Besides these the leaders can even revise their effectiveness according to the experiences and decisions of the peers and their seniors. As stated by one of the participant that experiences are best teachers irrespective of the fact that whether they are yours or someone else's. The key here is to learn the lessons and morals from them which would guide one on how to avoid the other problems. This could be a very good and practical approach for the leaders in order to be effective.

This study also carried out the task of gaining knowledge about the personal values that could affect the ethical decision making process of leaders. A number of personal values and principles came to surface as a result of this enquiry. One of the respondent very much influenced by religious values depicted that the decisions that he take do reflect his religious values but in balanced manner. Environment is another factor that could impact in the decision that a leader takes. Concluding it all, different factors and elements do affect the decision making process of the leaders. These factors included personal morals and religious values, interests of the stakeholders, vision and mission of the organization and most importantly the impact of the problem and its solution on the society influence the ethical decisions of leaders in general. During the course of interview, an important question was posed to the participants that aimed at acquiring knowledge about the problems that leaders face during an ethical dilemma. Responses received help in concluding that generally the situation of panic that arises de-focuses the employees and here the traits of a leader are tested about how they keep them motivated focused along with devising solutions for the problem. Another big issue that arises during decision making to resolve an ethical dilemma is to keep balance between the personal as well the organizational and the leadership values (McCartney & Campbell, 2006).

According to the responses received, it can be concluded that the personal nature of a person influences his daily dealings. For instance, if a person is results oriented then he would seek same approach in his daily practices. Same goes for leaders, like if a leader is result oriented then he would best fit within the environments of a mission oriented organizations. Considering it generally, an important characteristics of an ethical leader that his decisions do not pose difficulties for any one and all his decisions take into account the benefits and interests of the society. One of the best practices or approaches as revealed by the research conducted in this study is to include the consent of the team members before taking any major decision that includes their interests as well. This approach is likely to infuse sense of motivation in the employees and make them more dedicated to the mission and give their best for the accomplishments of the tasks. This approach will also make them and their opinions feel respected. Linking it all together, several personal and good traits like respecting others, sensitivity to the interests of others and society matters if incorporated within the leadership practices can make leaders educationally as well as ethically effective (Kouzes &Posner, 2002).

Concluding all the above provided discussion, it could be said that the leaderships is a matter of real competence. It involves such scenarios and situations that pose great challenges to the leaders. The best practices and the traits of a leader come under real test when he is faced with such an ethical quandary. In such situations personal morals, religious values and many other factors may influence the ethical decision making process of the leader. During such situation the art of balancing the situation and keeping the task force focused and motivated depends on the educational and ethical effectiveness of the leader himself. The leaders with the qualities like honesty, self estimation, creativity, integrity, truthfulness, selflessness, respect for others, sensitivity to the environment are real champions as they are best able to handle situations without being carried away by their psychological state of mind and devise balanced and proportionate decisions with the help of their best practices they adopt and best qualities they posses.

Strengths, weaknesses, and limitations of the research

Through the responses of the participants it was observed that the personal principles of a person influence his dealings and similar concept was provided in the study of Waggoner (2010). And it is also important fact that the principles and values of an individual may be altered as a result of the psychological and the social aspects. Therefore, a question was posed to the participants about the psychological and the social aspects that can endanger principles of individuals. It was concluded that the individual principles need to be in accordance with the cultural values of the particular society otherwise they cannot be practiced openly and without criticism. The cultural aspect of the region a person belongs to guides his basic morals and values. The personal values of a person are definitely influenced by their psychological state of mind. A person coming from a stable background will have firm moral values and principles rather than a psychologically disturbed person. The environment that person receives at his first school which is his home of course helps in making up the future morals and values that he will be practicing. In context of ethical decision making in leadership, the social and psychological aspects with the potential of endangering individual's principles are significant because inevitably the personal values of a person do get reflected in his leadership practices (Brown & Trevino, 2006).

Recommendations

The aim of this study was to conduct a research on the importance of ethical decision making of leaders and add to the unexplored aspects of previous work. This study provided a focused research material because the analysis of the research was based on responses collected from those individuals who perform leadership duties at different levels. The study forms a ground for future research in this direction to unveil further aspects. There are some recommendations for future studies to investigate the importance of ethical decision making for an effective leader in a further focused manner.

The analysis of this study is based on Ethnography Primary Qualitative Research. Adopting a quantitative methodology in future would help in analyzing the insight of people about the topic in a broad perspective. Another recommendation is categorizing the participants in accordance with their genders and ages. This would help in examining the difference of mindset of different age groups. This study is based on interview with a panel of those respondents who render services at leaders. So in future, those should also be analyzed who do not perform duties as leaders. This approach would help in investigating those aspects of effective and ethical leadership which are expected to be seen.

To discover further about the influence of social and psychological aspects of the ability of ethical decision making, categorical and quantitative research would be an appropriate idea. This will include leaders and workers from different social backgrounds. It is important that future studies must extend the previous work. Therefore it is recommended that those areas should be focused which are not investigated in detail in previous studies. For instance, this study has highlighted three pillars of ethical decision making which are honesty, integrity and truth. So it is recommended that further studies should conduct research on other less often discussed aspects.

References

Aaltio-Marjosola, I., & Takala, T. (2000) Charismatic leadership, manipulation and the complexity of organizational life, *Journal of Workplace Learning*, vol.12 (4), pp.146

Anderson, D.J. (2006) Qualitative and Quantitative research, p.3

Antonakis, J., Cianciolo, A. T., & Sternberg, R. J. (2004) *The Nature of Leadership*, Thousand Oaks, CA: Sage

Avolio, B. J., & Gardner, W. I. (2005) Authentic leadership development: Getting to the root of positive forms of leadership. *The Leadership Quarterly*, vol.16 (3), pp.315-338

Avolio, B. J., & Yammarino, F. J. (2002) Transformational and charismatic leadership: The road ahead. New York, NY: Elsevier.

Badaracco, J. (2002) Defining Moments: When managers must choose between right and right. *Boston: Harvard Business School Press*

Bajpai, B.R. & Singh K.Y. (2009) Research Methodology, Data Presentation

Beasley, M. S., &Hermanson, D. R. (2004) Going beyond Sarbanes-Oxley compliance: Five keys to creating value, *CPA Journal,* Vol. 74, pp. 11-13, New York State Society of CPA's

Beauchamp, T. L., & Bowie, N. E. (2004).Ethical theory and business (7th Ed.), Upper Saddle River, NJ: Pearson.

Begley, P. T., & Leithwood, K. A. (1990) The influence of values on school administrator practices. *Journal of personnel evaluation in education*, vol.3, pp.337-352

Bell, J. (2005) Embedding ethical frameworks in the leadership system of not-forprofits: The special case of volunteers, *Gale, Cengage Learning*

Bennis, W. G. (1984). The 4 competencies of leadership, *Training and Development Journal,*vol. 38 (8), pp.14-19

Bennis, W. G. (2000). Leadership theory and administrative behavior: The problem of authority. *Administrative Science Quarterly*, vol.4, pp.259-260

Beu, D., & Buckley, M. R. (2001).The hypothesized relationship between accountability and ethical behavior.Journal of Business Ethics, vol. 34 (1), p.57

Bird, C. (2005) *Social Psychology*, New York: D. Appleton-Century Company

Blakeley, K. (2007). *Leadership blind spots and what to do about them,* West Sussex: John Wiley & Sons, Ltd

Bloom, D. B. & Crabtree, F. B. (2006) The qualitative research interview, MEDICAL EDUCATION 2006; 40: 314-321

Boal, K. K. B., &Hooijberg, R. R. (2000) Strategic leadership research: Moving on. The Leadership Quarterly, 11(4), pp.515-549

Bolman, L. G., & Deal, T. E. (2003) 'Reframing organizations artistry, choice, and leadership', (3rd Ed), San Fransico, CA: Wiley, n.d

Brown, S., & Trevino, L. K. (2006) 'Ethical leadership: A review and future directions', The Leadership Quarterly vol.17 (6), pp. 595-616

Burke, F. (1999) Ethical decision-making: Global concerns, frameworks, and Approaches. *Public Personnel Management*, vol.28, pp.529

Burns, J. M. (2004) Ethics, the heart of leadership (2nd Ed.). Westport, CT: Praeger Publishers.

Burns, J. M. (2004). Foreword.In J. B. Ciulla (Ed.), Ethics, the heart of leadership (2nd Ed.). Westport, CT: Praeger Publishers.

Carlson, D. S., Kacmar, K. M., & Wadsworth, L. L. (2002) The impact of moral intensity dimensions of ethical decision making: Assessing the relevance of orientation. *Journal of Managerial Issues*, vol. 14, pp.15

Christensen, S. L., & Kohls, J. (2003) Ethical decision making in times of organizational crisis, *Business and Society*, vol.42, pp.328

Ciulla, J. B. (2004) Leadership ethics: Mapping the territory. In J. B. Ciulla& J. M. Burns (Eds.), Ethics, the heart of leadership (2nd Ed.), Westport, and CT: Praeger Publishers

Ciulla,B.J. (2003)Ethics and Leadership Effectiveness, pp.302, 307, data retrieved from http://www.ila-net. org/Members/Directory/DownloadS/Antonakis-Ciulla-13.pdf

Clarke, J.R. (2005) Research Models and Methodologies, p.1-45

Clawson, J. (2006) Level three leadership: Getting below the surface (6th ed.). Upper Saddle River, NJ: Pearson Prentice Hall.

Cohan, Peter S. (2004) *Value Leadership*: The 7 Principles that drive corporate value in an economy, San Francisco: Jossey-Bass.

Conger, J. A., &Kanungo, R. N. (1987).Toward a behavioral theory of charismatic leadership in organizational settings.Academy of Management.The Academy of Management Review, vol.12 (4), pp.637

Creswell, J., (2005), "Educational Research," 2nd edition, Upper Saddle River, NJ: Pearson Education, Inc, pp. 58-97

D'Aprix, A. S. (2005) Ethical decision-making models: A two-phase study. Unpublished 3177652, Case Western Reserve University, United States—Ohio

Day, G. S., & Shoemaker, P. J. (2006) Leading the vigilant organization. Strategy & Leadership, vol.34, pp.4-10

Delaney, J. T., &Sockell, D. (1992) Do company ethics training programs make a difference? An empirical analysil, *Journal of Business Ethics*, vol.11, pp.719-727

Fort, T. L. (1996) Religious belief, corporate leadership, and business ethics, American Business Law Journal, vol.33, p. 451

Fort, T. L. (1997) Religion and business ethics: The lessons of political morality. Journal of Business Ethics, vol.16, p. 263

Friedman, H. H., & Langbert, M. (2000) Abraham as a transformational leader, Journal of Leadership Studies, vol.7 (2), pp.88-95

Fulmer, R. M. (2004) 'The Challenge of Ethical Leadership', Organizational Dynamics, vol.33(3), pp. 307-317

George, J. M. (2003) Emotions and leadership: The role of emotional intelligence, Human *Relations*, vol.53 (3), pp.1027-1055

Gibelman, M., & Gelman, Sheldon R. (2000) Very Public Scandals: An Analysis of How and Why Nongovernmental Organizations Get in Trouble, *International Society for Third-Sector Research (ISTR) Fourth International Conference, Dublin, Ireland*

Gini, A. (2004) Moral leadership and business ethics.In J. B. Ciulla (Ed.), Ethics, the heart of leadership (2nd Ed., pp. 25-43) Westport, CT: Praeger Publishers

Hallinger, P. (2003) Leading Educational Change: reflections on the practice of instructional and transformational leadership, Cambridge Journal of Education, vol.33 (3), pp. 329-351.

Hancock, B. (2002) Trent Focus for Research and Development in Primary Health Care: An Introduction to Qualitative Research, pp.2-15

Harvey, M. E. O. (2001) The impact of organization ethical climate and ethical ideology on the propensity to create budgetary slack and job satisfaction, Nova Southeastern University, Fort Lauderdale-Davie, FL

Haughey, D. J. (2007) Ethical relationships between instructor, learner, and institution, *Open Learning*, vol.*22* (2), pp.139-147

Heifetz, R. A., &Linsky, M. (2004) When leadership spells danger, Educational Leadership, pp. 33-37

Hox, J.J. & Boeije,R. H. (2005) Dta Collection, Primary vs. Secondary, p.593-599, vol. 1

Jones, T. M. (1991). Ethical decision making by individuals in organizations: An issue contingent model. *Academy of Management Review*, vo.16, pp.366

Kelley, P. C., & Elm, D. R. (2003) The effect of context on the moral intensity of ethical issues: Revising Jones' issue-contingent model. *Journal of Business Ethics*, vol.48, pp.139

Kimberling, Linda, S. (2008) Ethical reasoning and transformational leadership: An investigation of public sector leaders, *Doctoral dissertation, Capella University.*

Kohlberg, L. (1969). Stage and sequence: The cognitive-developmental approach to socialization. In D. A. Goslin (Ed.), Handbook of socialization theory and research, pp. 347-480, Chicago, IL: Rand McNally

Kohlberg, L. (1976) Moral stages and moralization, In T. Lickona (Ed.), Moral development and behavior: Theory, research, and social issues. New York, NY: Holt, Rinehart, & Winston

Kotter, J. P. (2007) What leaders really do,' in R. Vecchio (ed.), Leadership: Understanding the Dynamics of Power and influence in Organizations, 2nd edition (*University of Notre Dame Press, Notre Dame*, IN), pp. 23-32

Kouzes, J. M., & Posner, B. Z. (2002) The leadership challenge (3rd ed.). San Francisco, CA: Jossey-Bass

Lee, Y., & Chang, H. (2006) Leadership style and innovation ability: An empirical study of Taiwanese wire and cable companies. Journal of American Academy of Business, vol.9 (2), pp.218-222

Leithwood, K. A., & Stager, M. (1989) Expertise in principals' problem solving, *Education Administration Quarterly*, vol.25 (2), pp.126-161

Lunday, J., & Barry, M. (2004).Connecting the dots between intentions, action and results: A multi-pronged approach to ethical decision making. *Ivey Business Journal Online*, vol.1

McCartney, W. W., & Campbell, C. R. (2006) 'Leadership, management, and derailment: A model of individual success and failure', Leadership & Organization Development Journal, 27, pp. 190-202

McMillan, J. H., & Schumacher, S. (1997). Research in education: A conceptual introduction (4th Ed.). New York, NY: Longman.

Miesing, P., & Preble, J. F. (1985) A comparison of five business philosophies, *Journal of Business Ethics,* 4, p.465

Milgram, S. (1963).Behavioral study of obedience, *Journal of Abnormal and Social Psychology*, vol. 67, pp.371-378

Morse, J. M. (2005). Evolving trends in qualitative research: Advances in mixed method design. Qualitative Health Research, 15, 583-585

Mullane, P.S. (2009) Ethics and Leadership, p.n.d.

Neuman, L., (2005) Social research methods: qualitative and quantitative approaches, 6th edition, Boston, PA: Allyn and Bacon, pp. 36-49

Onwuegbuzie, A., & Leech N., (2006), "Linking research questions to mixed methods data analysis procedures," The Qualitative Report, 11(3), pp. 474-498

Ostrower, David B. (2007) Nonprofit Governance in the United States, Washington, D.C.: *The Urban Institute.*

Paine, L. S. (1994) Managing for organizational integrity, Harvard Business Review, Vol. 72, pp. 106, Harvard Business School Publication Corp

Parry, K. (2004) Comparative Modeling of the Social Processes of Leadership in Work Units. *Journal of Management and Organization*

Parry, K. W., & Proctor-Thomson, S. B. (2002) Perceived integrity of transformational leaders in organisational settings, Journal of Business Ethics, vol.35 (2), p.75

Patton, Q. M. and Cochran, M. (2002) A Guide to Using Qualitative Research Methodology, pp.2-21

Polkinghorne, D. E. (2005) Language and meaning: Data collection in qualitative research. *Journal of Counseling Psychology*, vol.52 (2), pp.137-145

Reidenbach, R. E., & Robin, D. P. (1990) Toward the development of a multidimensional scale for improving evaluations of business ethics. Journal of Business Ethics, vol.9, pp.639-653

Reisman, J. (n.d.) A Handbook Of Data Collection Tools: Companion To "A Guide To Measuring Advocacy And Policy", pp.2-45

Resick, C.J., Hanges, P.J., Dickson, M.W., & Mitchelson, J. K. (2006) A cross-cultural examination of the endorsement of ethical leadership. *Journal of Business Ethics,vol.* 63(4), pp.345-359

Rest, James R. (1994) *Moral development: Advances in Research and Theory.* New York: Praeger Publishers, vol.26-39

Rhode, Deborah L. & Packel, Amanda K. (2009) Ethics and nonprofits, *Stanford Social Innovation Review*

Sankar, Y. (2003) Character not charisma is the critical measures of leadership excellence. *Journal of Leadership & Organizational Studies*, 9 (4), 45

Satterlee, A. (2009) Organizational Management and Leadership: A Christian Perspective, Synergistics Inc.

Spradley (1979) Appendix B: Ethnographic interviews and questions, p.n.d.

Starratt, R. J. (2004) *Ethical leadership,* San Francisco: Jossey-Bass

Trevino, L. K., & Brown, M. E. (2004) Managing to be ethical: Debunking five business ethics myths, *Academy of Management Executive*, vol.18 (2), pp.69-81
Trevino, L. K., Weaver, G. R., Gibson, D. G., & Toffler, B. L. (1999) Managing ethics and legal compliance: What works and what hurts. *California Management Review*, vol.41 (2), p. 131

Vitell, S. J., Dickerson, E. B., &Festervand, T. A. (2000) Ethical problems, conflicts and beliefs of small business professionals, *Journal of Business Ethics*, vol.28 (1), p.15

Waggoner, J. (2010) Ethics and Leadership: How Personal Ethics Produce Effective Leaders, pp.7-28

Weston, A. (2001). A 21st century ethical toolbox, New York, NY: *Oxford University Press*

Winget, M. (2004) Qualitative Research: The "Ethnography of Annotation" Model, pp.1-16

Wood, R., & Bandura, A. (1989).Social cognitive theory of organizational management.The Academy of Management Review, 14, 361.

Yukl, G. A., & Tracey, J. B. (1992) Consequences of influence tactics used by subordinates, peers, and the boss, *Journal of Applied Psychology*, vol.77 (4), pp.525-535

APPENDIX A

Questions asked during the study were:

1) How do you define leadership?
2) What is the real characteristic of a good leader?
3) Which forms of leadership are associated with educational effectiveness?
4) What is the importance of ethics in decision-making in organizations?
5) What are the psychological and the social aspects that can endanger individuals' principles?
6) Describe your leadership traits in relation with integrity, honesty, and trustworthiness?
7) What in your opinion helps in dealing with ethical dilemmas during ethical decision making process?
8) What are the factors that affect your ethical decision making process?
9) How your personal values affect your decision making process?
10) What sort of difficulties do you experience during an ethical decision making process?
11) What piece of advice would you give to future leaders to be an effective leader?

APPENDIX B

Interview Consent Form

Dear Participant,

The purpose of this research study is to explore the best practices of leadership and their educational effectiveness. You are being invited to participate in for the interview session conducted in context of the research as you are experienced and knowledgeable in this regard.

If you agree to participate your participation will last for approximately 2 hours. Your participation in this study is completely voluntary and you may refuse to participate at any time. Acknowledgement to this email indicates your willingness to participate. During the study you may expect the following procedures to be followed: You will be asked a few questions regarding leadership and its best practices.

To ensure confidentiality to the extent permitted by law, the following measures will be taken: 1) session will remain completely isolated and no personal identification will be asked 2) name of any person, if mentioned by you will not be published in the research, 3) only the identified researchers will have access to the study records 4) records will be kept in a locked office. There are no foreseeable risks at this time from participating in this study. You will not incur costs by participating in this study and you will not be compensated.

We hope the information gained in this study will benefit society, organizations by helping to identify maximum possible dimensions of adopting leadership practices during ethical dilemma and decision making processes.

Thank you for your assistance.

Sincerely,

[Your Name]
[Designation]
[Email Address]

APPENDIX C

	Resources	Research type	Consent Required	No. Of Sources
Secondary source	Online libraries for e.g. Proquest, EBSCO etc	Desk Research	No	More than 50 articles
Primary Source	Interview Session	Field Research	Yes	10 participants